Same Size

These  are the **same size**.

Look at the pictures in each box.
Circle the pictures that are the same size.

Same and Different

These ⭐⭐ are the **same**. This ⭐ is **different**.

Look at the pictures in each row.
Circle the picture that is different.

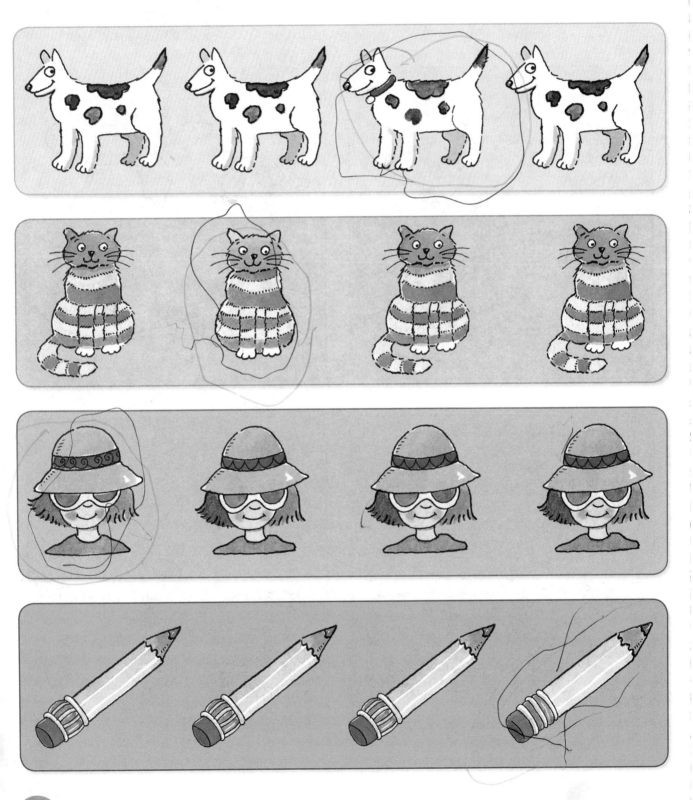

Big and Bigger

This  is **big**. This is **bigger**.

Look at the pictures in each row.
Circle the picture that is bigger than the first picture.

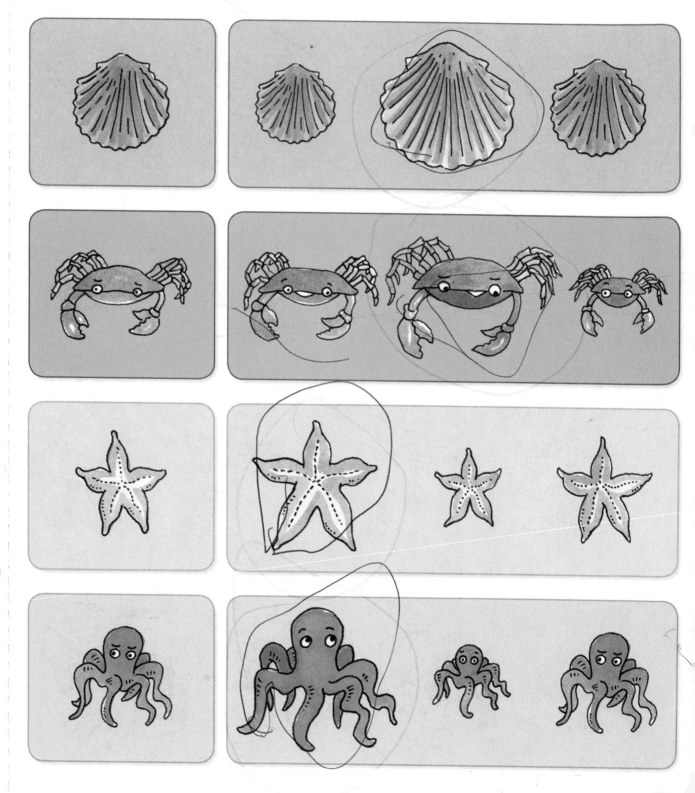

Small and Smaller

This is **small**. This is **smaller**.

Look at the pictures in each row.
Circle the picture that is smaller than the first picture.

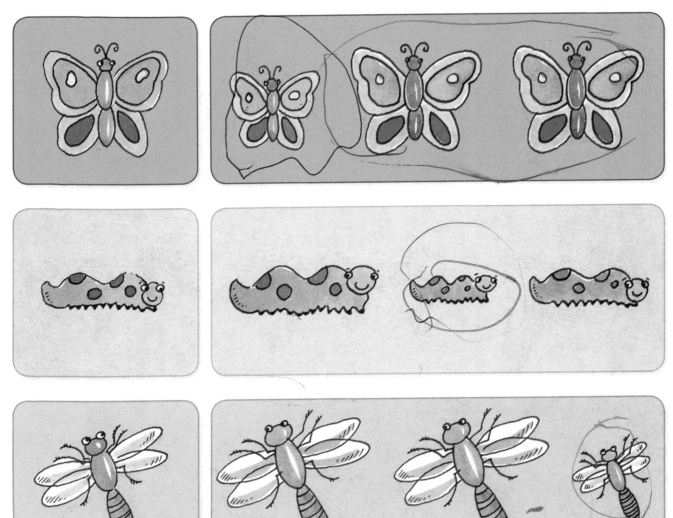

Draw lines to things that are almost the same, but **bigger**.

Comparing/Classifying

What Belongs Together?

Draw a line from each picture on the left to where it belongs.

What Belongs Together?

A  and 🔨 **belong** together.

Look at the pictures in each row.
Circle the picture that belongs with the first picture.

What Belongs Together?

Circle the names of the pictures in each row that belong together.

hat   bone   dog

shoe   sock   ball

bee   car   flower

bucket   bird   mop

What Belongs Together?

Draw a line from the  below to what belongs in it.

What Belongs Together?

Where does each animal belong?
Draw a line from each animal to its **home**.

© School Zone Publishing Company 06345

What Belongs Together?

Draw a line from the **food** to the .

Draw a line from the **toys** to the .

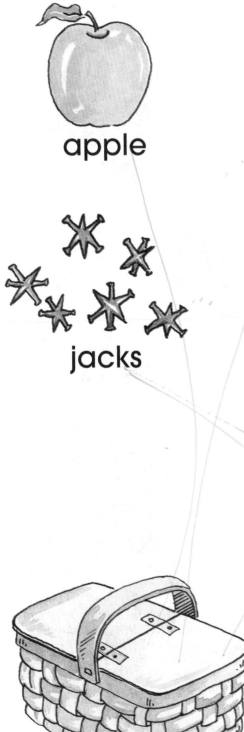

apple

berry

doll

jacks

ball

cake

What Belongs Together?

Draw a line from the  to the pictures that belong with it.

Which One Does Not Belong?

Cross out the one that **does not belong**.

Which One Does Not Belong?

Circle the name of the picture in each row that does not belong.

fork   fox   spoon

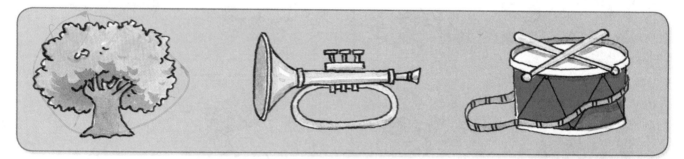

tree   horn   drum

bed   fan   pillow

box   bat   ball

Which One Does Not Belong?

Circle the name of the picture in each row that does not belong.

goat   pig   king

fish   house   barn

apple   bird   orange

hat   coat   cow

Animal Or Plant?

Write the names of the **animals** on the **left**.
Write the names of the **plants** on the **right**.

dog

fish

flower

bush

tree

cow

Animals	Plants
dogfish	bush
cow	tree
	flower

What Do You See?

Underline the sentence that **goes with** each picture.

See the ball.

See the dog.

See the doll.

See the ball.

See the boat.

See the dog.

See the doll.

See the boat.

On The Farm

Underline the sentences that tell you what you see.

There are two cows.

There are four balls.

There is a house.

There is one goat.

There is a girl.

Fur Or Feathers?

Most mammals have fur.

Birds have feathers.

Say each animal's name.

Circle ○ animals that have fur.

Check ✔ animals that have feathers.

Cross out ✗ animals that don't have fur or feathers.

rabbit

rooster

turtle

robin

cat

mouse

fish

parrot

puppy

How many have fur? _4_

How many have feathers? _3_

Lots Of Legs

Most mammals have four legs.

Birds have two legs.

Insects have six legs.

Say each animal's name.

Circle ○ the number of legs.

horse
0 2 4 6

hen
0 2 4 6

sheep
0 2 4 6

snake
0 2 4 6

pig
0 2 4 6

bee
0 2 4 6

cow
0 2 4 6

ant
0 2 4 6

goose
0 2 4 6

How many have four legs? ___4___   How many have six legs? ___3___

How many have two legs? ___2___   How many have no legs? ___1___

It's Only Natural

Things that are **natural** come from nature.
Things that are manufactured are **made by people**.

Circle ◯ things that are natural.

Cross out **X** things that are made by people.

Write A Riddle!

Draw one more thing that belongs in each group.

The Beach

towels   fins   goggles

A Picnic

drinks   dishes   food

Use two words from above to write a riddle.
Read the riddle to a friend.

_____

I am going somewhere. I will take some _____

_____

and some _____. Where am I going?

I'm going _____ To The Stors _____.

Putting Things Away

Read the story.
Do you put things away?
That makes them easy to find later.

Lisa puts her toys away.
She puts the art things in the art box.
She puts the toys in the toy box.
She puts books on the bookshelf.

Draw lines from the things to where they go.

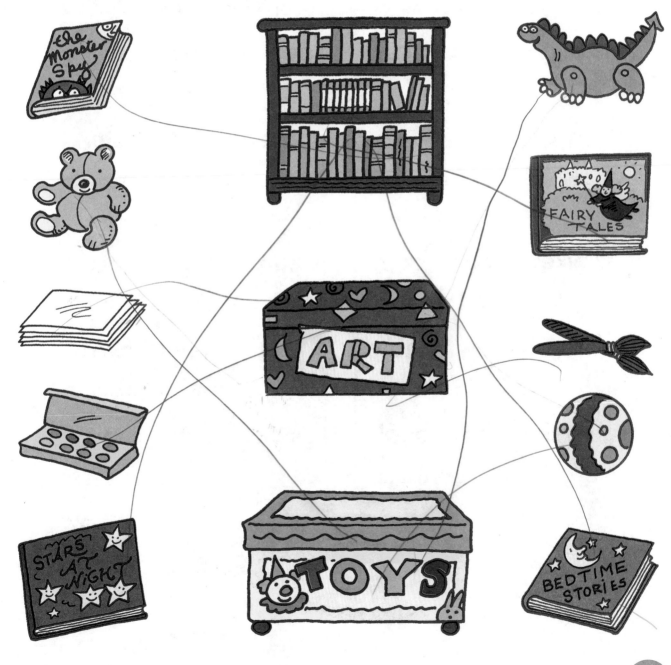

What Belongs Together?

Draw a line through the words that belong together.
Look across, down, and diagonally.

4

fish	key	five
bug	jump	four
star	blue	two

5

mom	hat	dog
penny	dad	sun
house	bird	sister

bike	moon	goat
run	cow	snow
duck	cat	book

sun	big	goat
wet	rain	two
star	old	snow

2

What Belongs Together?

Draw a line through the words that belong together.
Look across, down, and diagonally.

bee	ant	fly
seal	hat	frog
house	ball	blue

penny	cat	school
kite	beach	run
zoo	walk	red

blue	jump	hot
bed	dig	sit
hat	shoes	jeans

drum	owl	lizard
wolf	apple	turtle
boot	crab	snake

on   by   under

Draw a red 🍎 **under** the 🪑.

Draw a green 🍏 **on** the 🪑.

Draw a yellow 🍎 **by** the 🪑.

Write the correct number on each line.

How many 🐱 are **under** the 🪑 ? _3_

How many 🌼 are **in** the 🏺 ? _5_

How many 🐱 are **on** the 🪑 ? _3_

Over, By, In, or Under?

over

by

in

under

Write the word that tells **where** the bird is.

The bird is _____ under _____ the .

Over, By, In, or Under?

The bird is ___*over*___ the .

The bird is ___*by*___ the.

The bird is ___*in*___ the.

What Letter Comes Next?

Fill in each blank with the letter that comes **next** in ABC order.

A B C D E F G H I J K L M N O P Q R S T U V W X Y Z

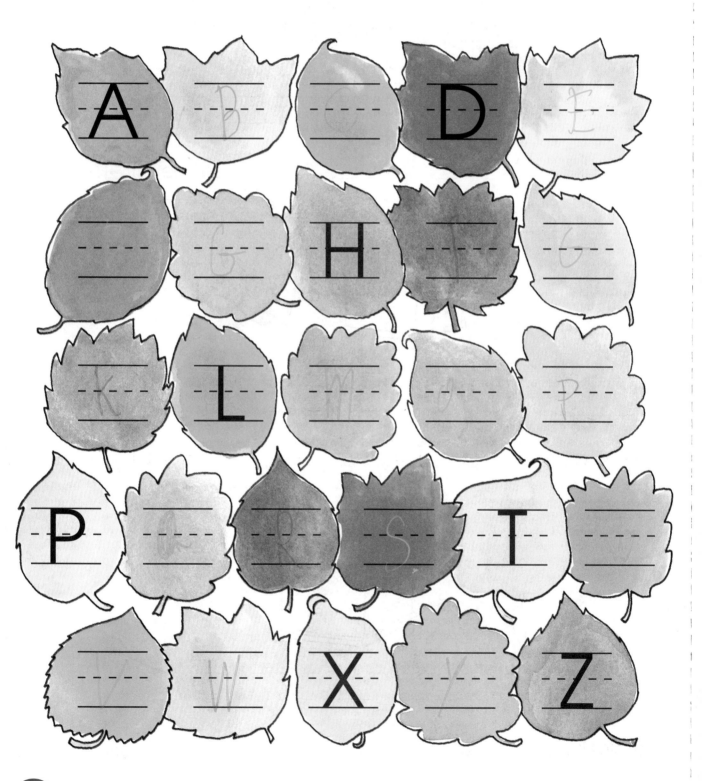

A comes **before** B.

Write the letter that comes before each letter below.

A B C D E F G H I J K L M N O P Q R S T U V W X Y Z

B comes **between** A and C.

Write the letter that comes between the letters below.

A B C D E F G H I J K L M N O P Q R S T U V W X Y Z

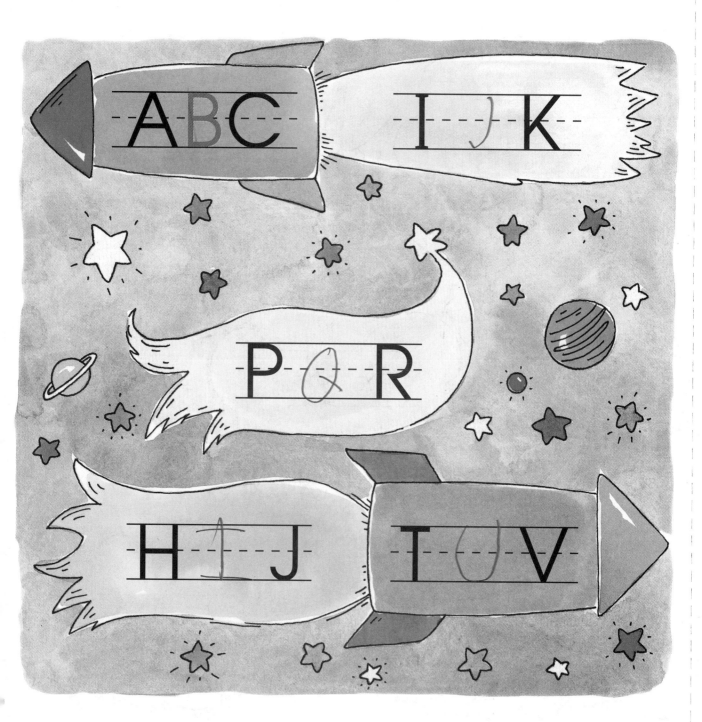

C comes **after** B.

Write the letter that comes after each letter below.

A B C D E F G H I J K L M N O P Q R S T U V W X Y Z

Write each set of letters in ABC order.

A B C D E F G H I J K L M N O P Q R S T U V W X Y Z

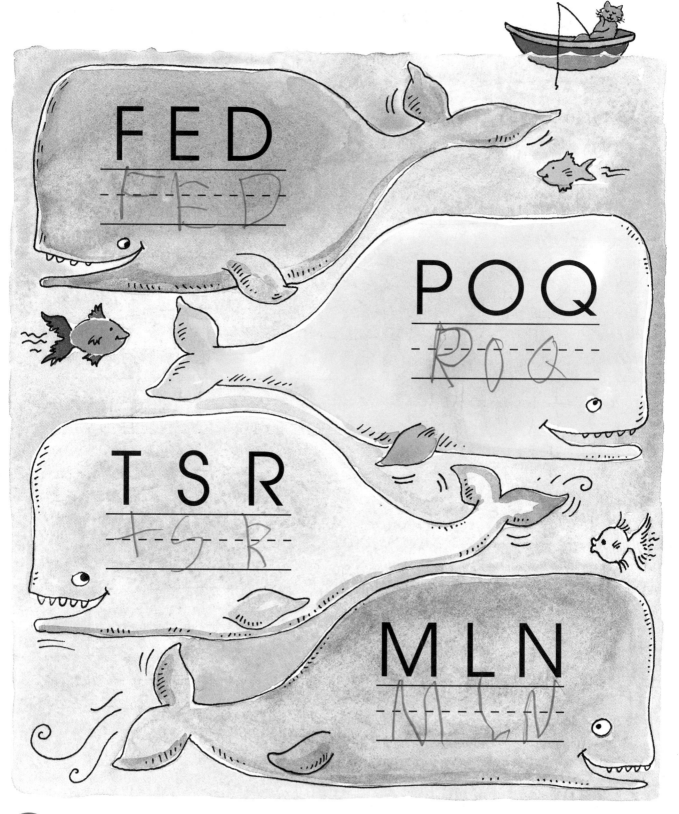

FED
FED

POQ
ROQ

TSR
TSR

MLN
MLN

Letter Match

Look at the ball players. Draw a line from each **uppercase** letter to the matching **lowercase** letter.

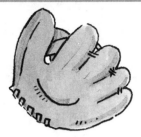

A B C D E F G H I J K L M N O P Q R S T U V W X Y Z

a b c d e f g h i j k l m n o p q r s t u v w x y z

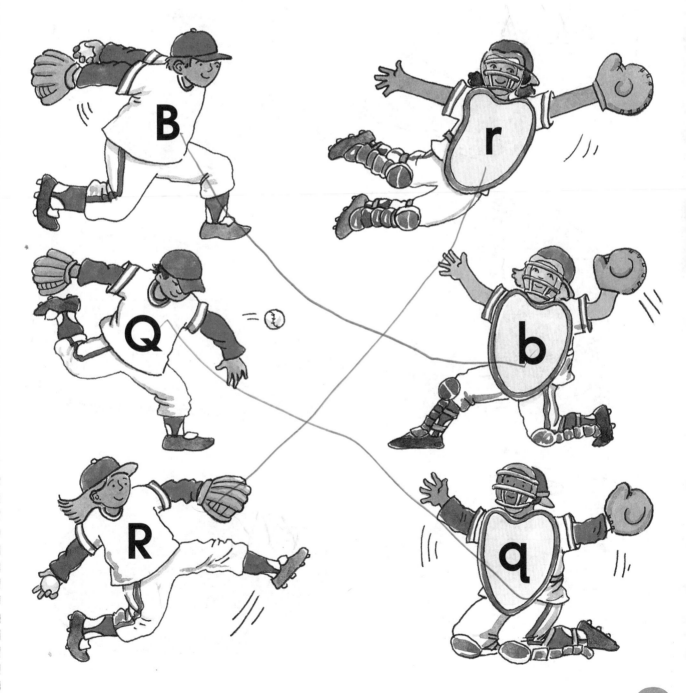

B

r

Q

b

R

q

Write the matching lowercase letter next to each uppercase letter.

A B C D E F G H I J K L M N O P Q R S T U V W X Y Z
a b c d e f g h i j k l m n o p q r s t u v w x y z

Write the words in ABC order.

A B C D E F G H I J K L M N O P Q R S T U V W X Y Z

a b c d e f g h i j k l m n o p q r s t u v w x y z

cat   bat   egg   dog   apple

apple ABcbefGHiJklm

NOparstuparstu

vwxyand

Write the words in ABC order.

A B C D E F G H I J K L M N O P Q R S T U V W X Y Z

a b c d e f g h i j k l m n o p q r s t u v w x y z

elf   fox   duck   goat   car

car car car car

elf elf elf elfelf elf

Fox Fox Fox Fox

duck duck duck

goat goat goat goat

Opposites

This 😀 is happy. This 😟 is sad.

Happy is the **opposite** of sad.

Draw a line from each word to the picture of its opposite.

little

night

up

Circle the picture that shows the opposite of the first picture.

big

soft

full

hot

Look at the word box. Circle the words in the puzzle.

stop go on off wet
dry hot cold up down

Opposites

Read the clues to finish the puzzle.

cold down go
left lost out

Across

1. found
3. hot
5. in

Down

1. right
2. stop
4. up

Opposites

Look at the word box. Circle the words in the puzzle.

in out new old
fast slow big little

Opposites

Read the clues to finish the puzzle.

down in day hot
run out happy

Across

2. up
3. sad

Down

1. walk
2. night
3. cold

Opposites

Read the clues to finish the puzzle.

Across

1. The opposite of new is __old__.
3. The opposite of fast is __slow__.
4. The opposite of day is __night__.

old short down
night slow near

Down

2. The opposite of up is __down__.
3. The opposite of long is __short__.
4. The opposite of far is __short__.

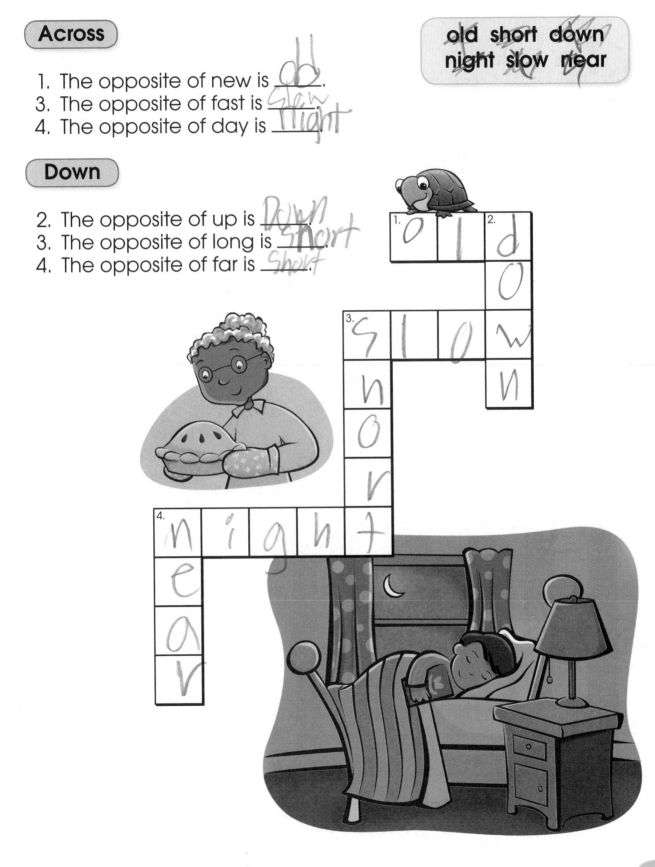

Left And Right

Write opposites of the words in Bear's and Hare's sacks.
Each pair of answers rhymes.

I'm left!

sad   full   little
wrong   drop   right
below

slow   I'm right!
bad   stop   pull
long   night
late

left
right

big
littel

above
below

catch
drop

correct
wrong

happy
sad

empty
full

day
night

early
late

fast
slow

go
stop

short
long

good
bad

push
pull

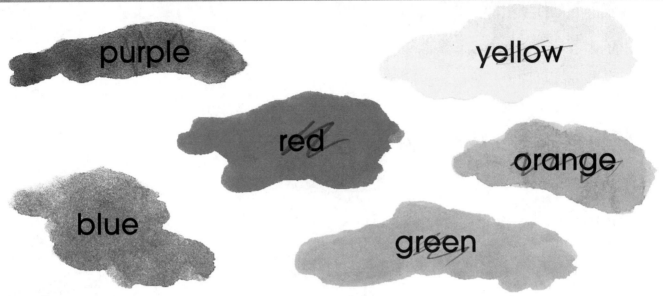

purple

yellow

red

orange

blue

green

Write the color words that fit the shapes.

orange   yellow

purple   green

red   blue

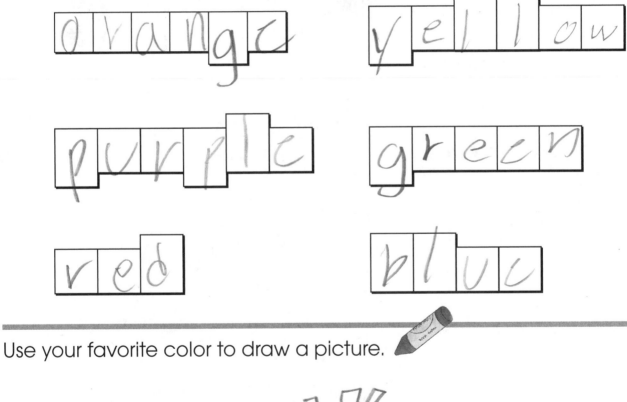

Use your favorite color to draw a picture.

Color The Picture

Color the 🌿 green.

Color the 🥚 yellow.

Color the 🐟 blue.

Color the 🌿 purple.

Color the ⭐ orange.

Color the 🦦 brown.

Color the 🚢 red.

Color the 🪨 black.

Color the ☁ white.

Get Through The Maze!

Help put the crayons away. Follow the directions.

Make a **red** line to put the **red** crayon away.
Make a yellow line to put the yellow crayon away.
Make a **blue** line to put the **blue** crayon away.
Make a **green** line to put the **green** crayon away.

Finish the sentence by writing the name of your favorite color.

My favorite color is

yellow

© School Zone Publishing Company 06345

Find The Message!

Follow the directions.
Then read the words that are left.

Color the **Y** boxes **red**.

Color the **C** boxes **blue**.

Color the **J** boxes orange.

Color the **H** boxes **purple**.

Color the **Z** boxes green.

Y	I	C	J	Z	L	I	K	E	C
R	E	D	C	J	Z	Y	H	J	Y
H	Z	Y	F	L	O	W	E	R	S
A	N	D	Y	P	U	R	P	L	E
C	J	B	A	L	L	O	O	N	S.

Write the words. Show the message to someone.

Look at the word box. Circle the words in the puzzle.

red blue black green
yellow orange purple

```
y e l l o w f m p
n v a p j h v k u
v w g r e e n w r
o m z l h k c f p
r w b l u e n t l
a m x c v s p j e
n k x r e d v w s
g m n f d c p k w
e n v h b l a c k
```

Learn The Shapes

Learn the shapes by tracing the dotted lines.

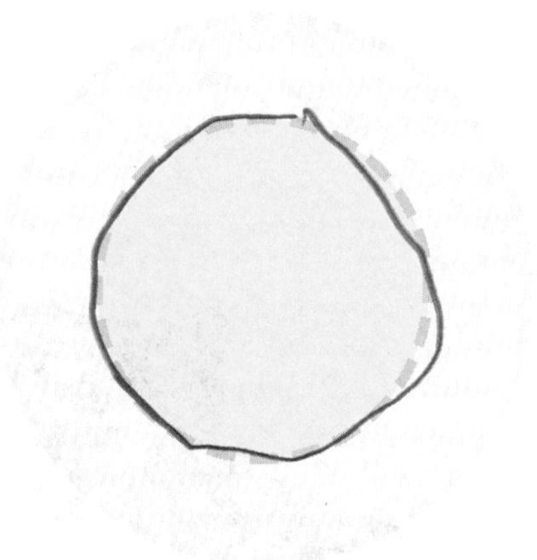

circle

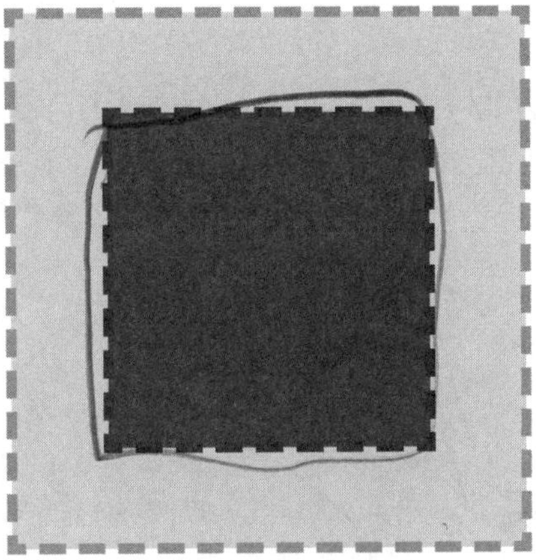

square

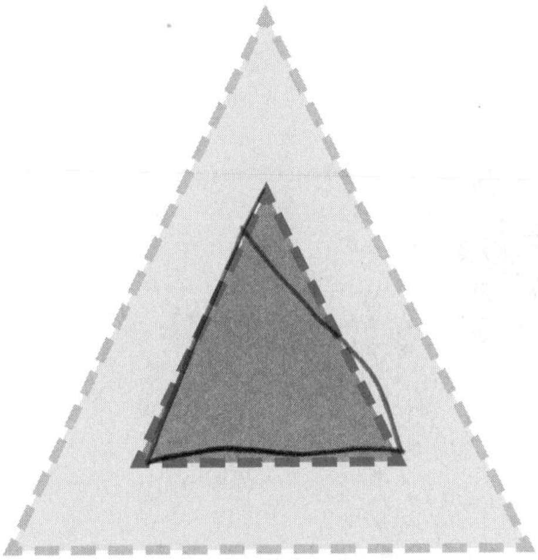

triangle

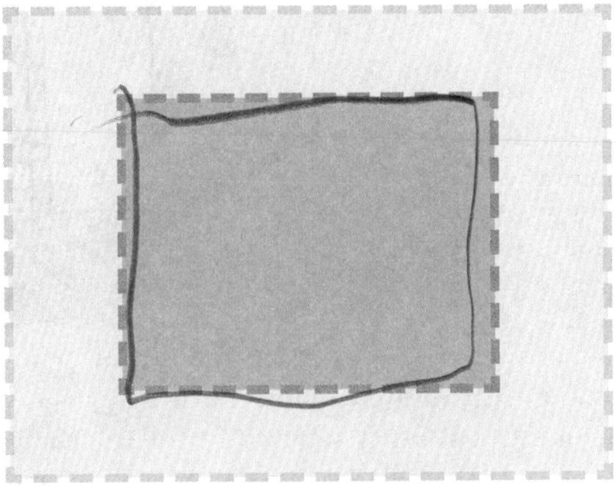

rectangle

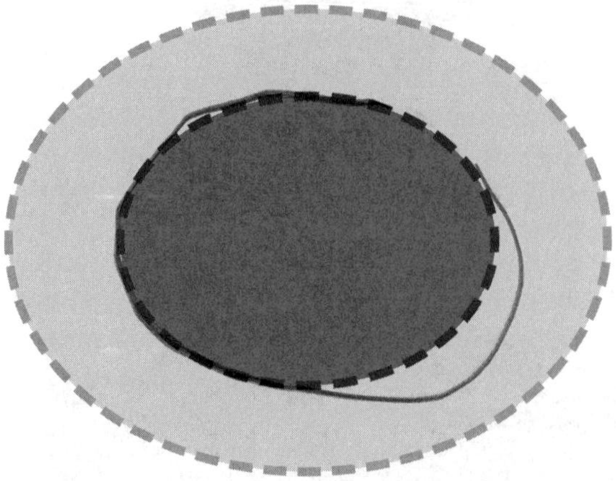

oval

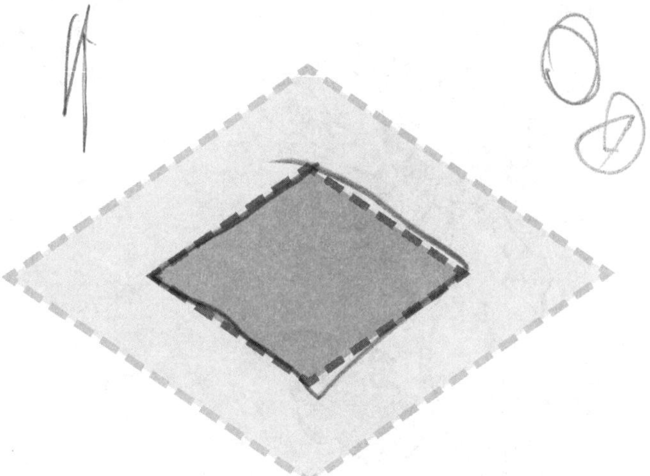

diamond

What Is A Circle?

A **circle** is a shape that looks like this. ◯

How many ◯ can you find? _____

What Is A Square?

A **square** is a shape that looks like this. ☐

How many ☐ can you find? _____

A **triangle** is a shape that looks like this.

How many can you find? ___7___

A **rectangle** is a shape that looks like this. ☐

How many ☐ can you find? _1_

Words That Describe Shapes

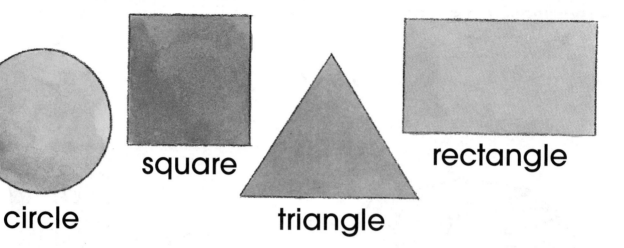

circle

square

triangle

rectangle

Read the riddles.
Write the answers.

I have three sides.

triangle

I have four sides that are the same length.

Square

I am round.

circle

I have four sides.
Two pairs are the same length.

rectangle

Shipshape Garden

Circle the shape for each part of the garden.

corn		triangle	rectangle	square
carrots		triangle	rectangle	square
peas		triangle	rectangle	square
radishes		Triangle	rectangle	square
beans		triangle	rectangle	square

Say the word. Then write the word.

all   _all_

Write the word **all** to complete the sentence.

Lisa keeps   _all_   her money in a piggy bank.

Write the word **all** to complete each sentence.

Lisa took _____ _all_ _____ her money out of the piggy bank.

She put _____ _all_ _____ the pennies in a pile.

She put _____ _all_ _____ the nickels in a pile.

She put _____ _all_ _____ the dimes in a pile.

How much money does she have in _____ _all_ _____ ?

Write the letters **b**, **t**, and **c** to finish the words.
Say each word.

_b_ all   _c_ all   _t_ all

the word.

Write the word **and** to complete the sentence.

_____

Jack _____ Jill went up the hill.

Write the word **and** between the matching pictures.

Jack _____ Jill

shoes _____ socks

cookies _____ milk

hat _____ coat

cat _____ dog

Write the letters **l**, **s**, and **h** to finish the words.
Say each word.

_____ and   _____ and   _____ and

Say the word. Then write the word.

at _____

Write the word **at** to complete the sentence.

_____

Mom is _____ home.

Draw a line connecting the words that end with the letters **at**.

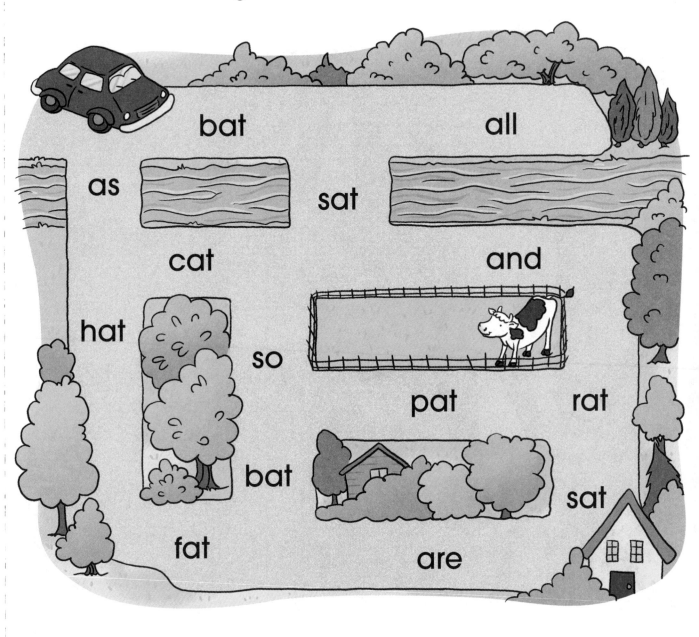

bat

all

as

sat

cat

and

hat

so

bat

pat

rat

fat

are

sat

Write the letters **c**, **h**, and **s** to finish the words.
Say each word.

_ _ at   _ _ at   _ _ at

Say the word. Then write the word.

big _____

Write the word **big** to complete the sentence.

_____

An elephant is _____ .

Write the word **big** under the **big** animals.

Write the letters **b**, **p**, and **d** to finish the words.
Say each word.

__ ig   __ ig   __ ig

Say the word. Then write the word.

can _____

Write the word **can** to complete the sentence.

_____

Nick _____ ride a bike.

Write the word **can** to complete each sentence.

_____

Nick _____ ride a bike.

_____

He _____ make the bike go fast.

_____

He _____ make the bike slow down.

_____

He _____ make the bike stop.

_____

_____ you ride a bike?

Write the letters **c**, **f**, and **r** to finish the words.
Say each word.

____ an   ____ an   ____ an

Say the word. Then write the word.

come _____

Write the word **come** to complete the sentence.

_____

Can you _____ with us?

Circle the words that say **come**.

come	town	little
some	come	all
come	some	down
little	come	big
down	little	come

How many did you find? _____

Write the letters **s** and **c** to finish the words.
Say each word.

___ ome   ___ ome

Say the word. Then write the word.

down _____

Write the word **down** to complete the sentence.

_____

Benny fell _____ .

Write the word **down** to show what is going **down**.

Write the letters **d**, **g**, and **t** to finish the words.
Say each word.

_____ own   _____ own   _____ own

Say the word. Then write the word.

fun _____

Write the word **fun** to complete the sentence.

_____

The circus is _____.

Find the balloons that have the word **fun**. Color them red.

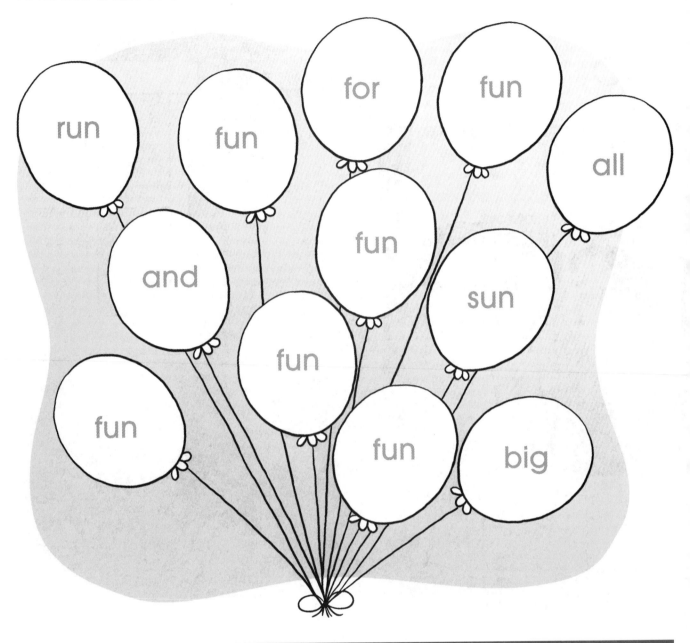

Write the letters **f**, **s**, and **r** to finish the words.
Say each word.

_____ un   _____ un   _____ un

Say the word. Then write the word.

go _____

Write the word **go** to complete the sentence.

_____

Where did Hero _____?

Draw a line connecting the words that say **go**.

go

go

so

to

go

go

go

see

can

go

go

go

go

Write the letters **g**, **n**, and **s** to finish the words.
Say each word.

Say the word. Then write the word.

had _____

Write the word **had** to complete the sentence.

_____

Ellie _____ fun at the park.

Draw a line through the words that say **had**.

bat	to	had
big	had	sad
had	can	he

has	sad	his
had	had	had
dad	the	her

Write the letters **h**, **s**, and **d** to finish the words.
Say each word.

____ ad   ____ ad   ____ ad

He Did It!

Say the word. Then write the word.

he _____

Write the word **he** to complete the sentence.

_____

Can _____ hit the ball?

Draw a line through the words that say **he**.

Start — ~~he~~	~~he~~	at	in
be	he	us	see
do	he	he	by
her	up	he	he

Finish

Write the letters **h**, **w**, and **b** to finish the words.
Say each word.

___ e   ___ e   ___ e

Say the word. Then write the word.

her _____

Ms. CLA.

Write the word **her** to complete the sentence.

Meg lost _____ mittens.

Write the word **her** to complete each sentence.

_____

Meg lost _____ mittens.

_____

Did _____ dog take them?

_____

Did _____ sister take them?

_____

Help Meg find _____ mittens.

Find Meg's mittens in the picture.
Color the picture.

You've Got It!

Say the word. Then write the word.

it

Color the words that say **it**.

Write the word **it** to complete the sentence.
What is the picture? Write the answer on the line.

What is _____ ?

Write the word **it** to complete each sentence.

_____

What is _____ ?

_____

Is _____ a toy?

_____

Is _____ a book?

_____

Is _____ a pet?

_____

Will I like _____ ?

Write the word **it** to complete the sentence.
Read the sentence.

_____

I like _____ .

Stay In Shape

Say the word. Then write the word.

in _____

Write the word **in** to complete the sentence.

_____

What is _____ the box?

Draw a line through the words that say **in**.

Start **in**	he	at	us	out
in	**in**	by	of	is
do	**in**	**in**	**in**	at
her	up	sat	**in**	**in**
pin	to	be	he	**in**

Finish

Write the letters **w**, **p**, and **t** to finish the words.
Say each word.

___ in   ___ ___ in   ___ ___ in

Say the word. Then write the word.

like _____

Write the word **like** to complete the sentence.

_____

I _____ ice cream.

Write the word **like** to complete each sentence.

_____

I _____ hot dogs.

_____

I _____ pizza.

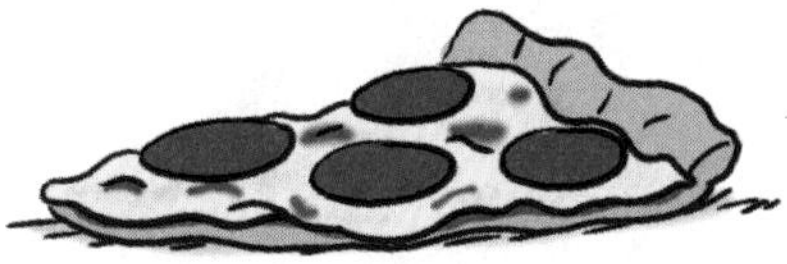

_____

I _____ pie.

_____

I _____ popcorn.

_____

I do not _____ peas.

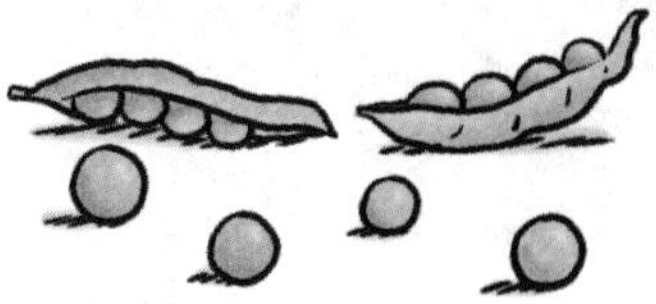

Write the letters **b**, **h**, and **l** to finish the words.
Say each word.

___ ike   ___ ike   ___ ike

Little Buddy

Say the word. Then write the word.

little _____

Write the word **little** to complete the sentence.

_____

I want the _____ one.

Write the word **little** to complete each sentence.

_____

A bird is _____ .

_____

A fish is _____ .

_____

A puppy is _____ .

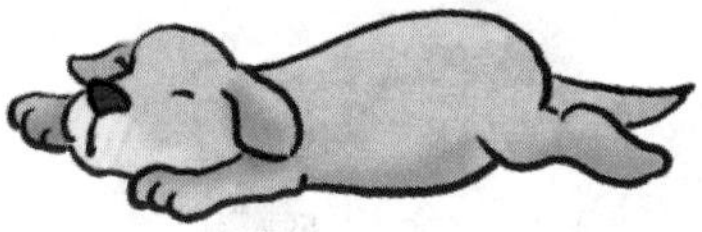

_____

A kitten is _____ .

Draw a picture of something that is **little**.

Look Around!

Say the word. Then write the word.

look _____

Write the word **look** to complete the sentence.

_____

Help me _____ for Fluff.

Draw a line through the words that say **look**.

Start	look	he	at	in
	look	look	look	see
	do	he	look	by
	her	up	look	look

Finish

Write the letters **l**, **b**, and **t** to finish the words.
Say each word.

_ _ _ ook   _ _ ook   _ _ ook

Say the word. Then write the word.

make _____

Write the word **make** to complete the sentence.

_____

Did you _____ this?

Draw a line through the words that say **make**.

make	lake	that
snake	make	bake
rake	cake	make

snake	lake	take
make	make	make
rake	cake	stake

Write the letters **b**, **t**, and **c** to finish the words.
Say each word.

_____ ake   _____ ake   _____ ake

Say the word. Then write the word.

me _____

Write the word **me** to complete the sentence.

_____

Can you come with _____ ?

Draw a line through the words that say **me**.

Start

me	he	at	us	out
me	me	by	of	she
do	me	me	me	at
her	up	sat	me	in
pin	to	be	me	me

Finish

Write the letters **m**, **h**, and **b** to finish the words.
Say each word.

_ _ e   _ _ e   _ _ e

Say the word. Then write the word.

on _____

Write the word **on** to complete the sentence.

_____

Oh, oh! The cat is _____ the table.

Circle the words that say **on**.

on

in   on

or

out   do

no

on

of   on   on   on

on

so   in

on

out

How many did you find? _____

Write the letters **R** and **D** to finish the names.
Say each name.

____ on   ____ on

Say the word. Then write the word.

play _____

Write the word **play** to complete the sentence.

_____

Let's _____ ball.

Circle the words that say **play**.
Say each word.

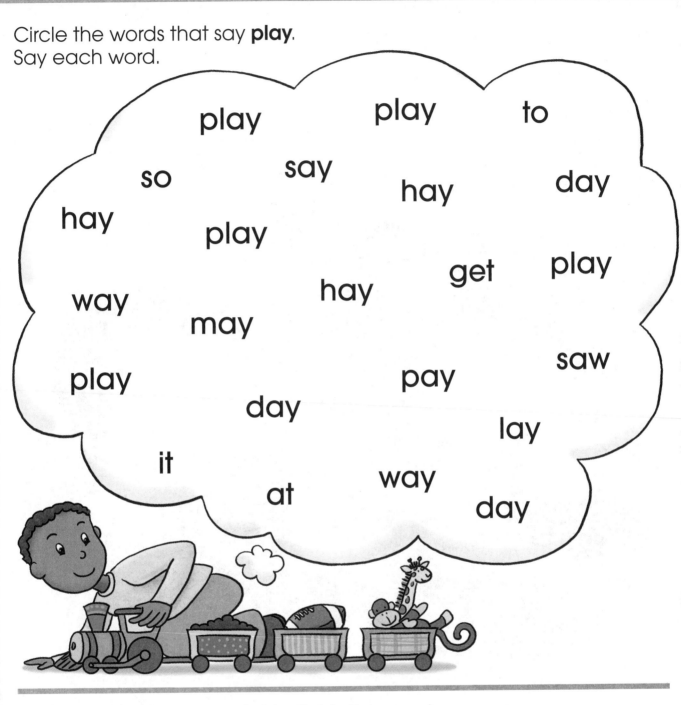

play   play   to

so   say   hay   day

hay   play   get   play

way   hay

may

play   day   pay   saw

it   lay

at   way   day

Write the letters **h**, **s**, and **d** to finish the words.
Say each word.

___ ay   ___ ay   ___ ay

In The Long Run

Say the word. Then write the word.

run _____

Write the word **run** to complete the sentence.

How fast can he _____?

Draw a line through the words that say **run**.

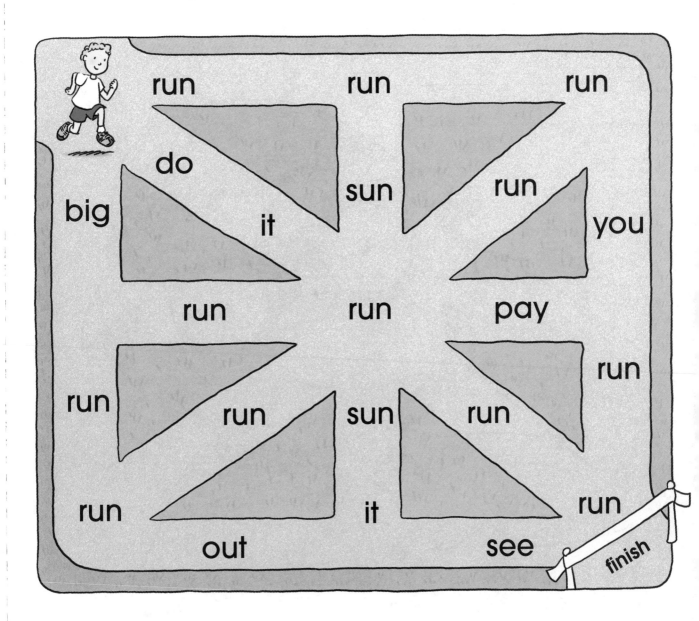

Write the letters **r**, **s**, and **f** to finish the words.
Say each word.

___ un   ___ un   ___ un

Say the word. Then write the word.

see _____

Write the word **see** to complete the sentence.

What do you _____ ?

Write the word **see**.
Draw a picture of something you can **see**.

_____

I_____ a

_____

I_____ a

_____

I_____ a

Write the letters **s** and **b** to finish the words.
Say each word.

___ ee   ___ ee

Pit Stop

Say the word. Then write the word.

stop _____

Write the word **stop** to complete the sentence.

A red light means _____.

Write the word **stop** to complete the sentence.

_____

I always _____ and look both ways.

Color the stop signs red.
How many did you find? _____

Say the word. Then write the word.

this _____

Write the word **this** to complete the sentence.

_____

Take _____ with you.

Color the flowers that say **this**.

How many did you find? _____

Say the word. Then write the word.

that _____

Write the word **that** to complete the sentence.

_____

What is _____ ?

© School Zone Publishing Company 06345

Draw a line through the words that say **that**.

sat	mat	that
cat	that	fat
that	this	the

snake	that	sat
this	that	make
mat	that	fat

Write the word **that** to complete the sentence.

_____

Is _____ a robot?

Who Are They?

Say the word. Then write the word.

they _____

Write the word **they** to complete the sentence.

_____

Did _____ find gold?

Draw a line connecting the words that say **they**.

Up, Up, And Away

Say the word. Then write the word.

up _____

Write the word **up** to complete the sentence.

_____

Look _____ to see falling leaves.

Color the leaves that say **up**.

When, Where, And Why

Say the word. Then write the word.

when _____

Write the word **when** to complete the sentence.

_____

I use this _____ it rains.

Circle the words that say **when**.

what   when

at   when   say   when

when   sun   when   then

when   when   run   when

when   what   when   who

How many did you find? _____

Who Knows?

Say the word. Then write the word.

who _____

Write the word **who** to complete the sentence.

_____

Do you know _____ he is?

Write the word **who** to complete each sentence.

_____

I know _____ is the doctor.

_____

I know _____ is the firefighter.

_____

I know _____ is the police officer.

_____

I know _____ is the teacher.

Who is each person?
Draw a line to show **who** they are.

Say the word. Then write the word.

you _____

Write the word **you** to complete the sentence.

How old are _____ ?

Write the word **you** to complete each sentence.

_____

We think _____ did a good job.

_____

Now _____ know more words.

_____

This will help _____ read.

_____

I know _____ like to read.

_____

What kind of books do _____ like best?

First, Next, Last

Write **1** in the square to show what happened **first**.
Write **2** to show what happened **next**.
Write **3** to show what happened **last**.

First, Next, Last

Write **1** in the square to show what happened **first**.
Write **2** to show what happened **next**.
Write **3** to show what happened **last**.

First, Next, Last

Write **1** in the square to show what happened **first**.
Write **2** to show what happened **next**.
Write **3** to show what happened **last**.

First, Next, Last

Write **1** in the square to show what happened **first**.
Write **2** to show what happened **next**.
Write **3** to show what happened **last**.

First, Next, Last

Write **1** in the square to show what happened **first**.
Write **2** to show what happened **next**.
Write **3** to show what happened **last**.

What's Next?

Draw what happens **next**.

It is time to cool off.

It is time to play.

It is time for lunch.

The sun gets hot.

Getting A Pet

Read the picture story.

Do you want a dog? Go to a pet store. Pick out a dog.

Take your dog home.

What will you name your dog?

Show how to buy a pet.
Number the pictures from **1** to **4** to show the correct order.

Pick out a pet.

Take your pet home.

Go to a pet store.

Name your pet.

Making A Sandwich

Read how to make a sandwich.

Ham and Cheese Sandwich Recipe
What you need: two pieces of bread, some ham, some cheese
1. Get two pieces of bread.
2. Put some ham on one piece.
3. Put some cheese on the ham.
4. Put the other slice of bread on top.
5. Eat!

Show how to make a sandwich.
Number the pictures from **1** to **4** to show the correct order.

Beginning Sounds

Circle the picture that begins with the same sound as the first one.

© School Zone Publishing Company 06345

Beginning Sounds

Circle the picture that begins with the same sound as the first one.

Dd doll

Zz zipper

Ll leaf

Rr rug

Beginning Sounds

Circle the picture that begins with the same sound as the first one.

Beginning Sounds

Circle the picture that begins with the same sound as the first one.

Yy yarn

Ww web

Tt top

Mm mittens

Beginning Sounds

Circle the picture that begins with the same sound as the first one.

Cc cow

Gg goose

Hh hat

Qq quarter

Xx x-ray

Say the name of each picture.
Write **t** or **n** to begin the word.
Then write the word on the line.

____op

____ent

____est

____ut

Beginning Sounds

Say the name of each picture.
Write **m** or **p** to begin the word.
Then write the word on the line.

____oon

____ig

____an

____an

Say the name of each picture.
Write **d** or **t** to end the word.
Then write the word on the line.

be____

_____

_____

goa____

_____

_____

ca____

_____

_____

bir____

_____

_____

Ending Sounds

Say the name of each picture.
Write **m** or **n** to end the word.
Then write the word on the line.

su____

gu____

_____

_____

_____

_____

dru____

fa____

_____

_____

Rhyming Pictures

 **rhymes** with .

Say the name of each picture.
Circle the two that **rhyme** in each group.

Rhyming Words 139

Draw lines to match the rhyming words.

mouse

star

car

house

cat

boat

goat

hat

Rhyming Words

Read the clues to finish the puzzle.

Across

2. It rhymes with lake _____.
3. It rhymes with back _____.
4. It rhymes with best _____.

Down

1. It rhymes with house _____.
2. It rhymes with clock _____.
3. It rhymes with twin _____.

mouse bake block
sack spin nest

Getting There

Summer is a good time to travel. People go from place to place across the country. What different kinds of transportation do they use?

Read each rhyme. Then write the type of transportation each rhyme describes.

I rhyme with hike. _____

I rhyme with us. _____

I rhyme with star. _____

I rhyme with pet. _____

I rhyme with plane. _____

Rhyme Time

Complete each poem with a word that rhymes.

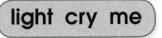

light cry me

Some animals hop.
Some animals fly.
Do some animals laugh?
Do some animals _____?

_____

_____

I like to read books,
while I'm in bed at night.
When I get sleepy,
I just turn out the _____.

_____

_____

My dog runs after squirrels
that climb up a tree.
He can't reach them,
so he runs back to _____.

_____

_____

Seasons

Complete each poem with a word that rhymes.

> **day   round   Spring**

I like the flowers growing.
I like the birds that sing.
I like the growing season.
We call that season _____.

_____

I like sunny days with
snow on the ground.
And I like the nights
when the moon is so _____.

_____

Some days are foggy.
Some days are gray.
But I like the times
when it's sunny all _____.

A short vowel makes a different sound.

cat   bed   pin   top   bug

Look at the pictures. Say the words.
Write the missing short vowels in the puzzle.

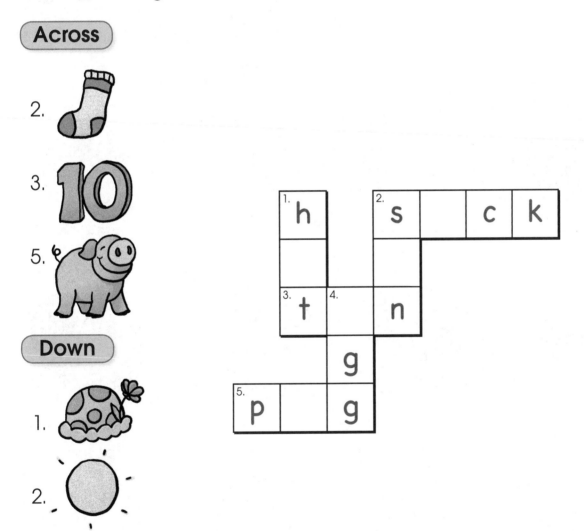

Across

2.

3.

5.

Down

1.

2.

4.

Words With Short a

Say each picture word.
Circle two **short a** pictures in each row.

short a sound
hat

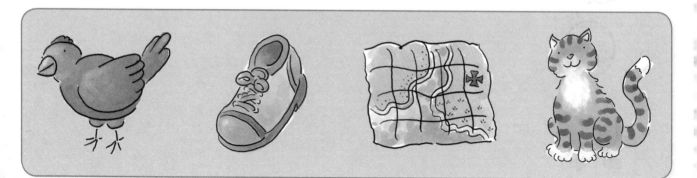

© School Zone Publishing Company 06345

Use the code to write the short a words.

nap man pat
mat bat cat

a   p   n   m   t

Write the words that go with the pictures.

Words With Short a

Put a letter in place of each number to finish the sentence.

> cat Dad hat
> sat bad mad

1	2	3	4	5	6	7	8	9
D	d	b	a	m	c	t	s	h

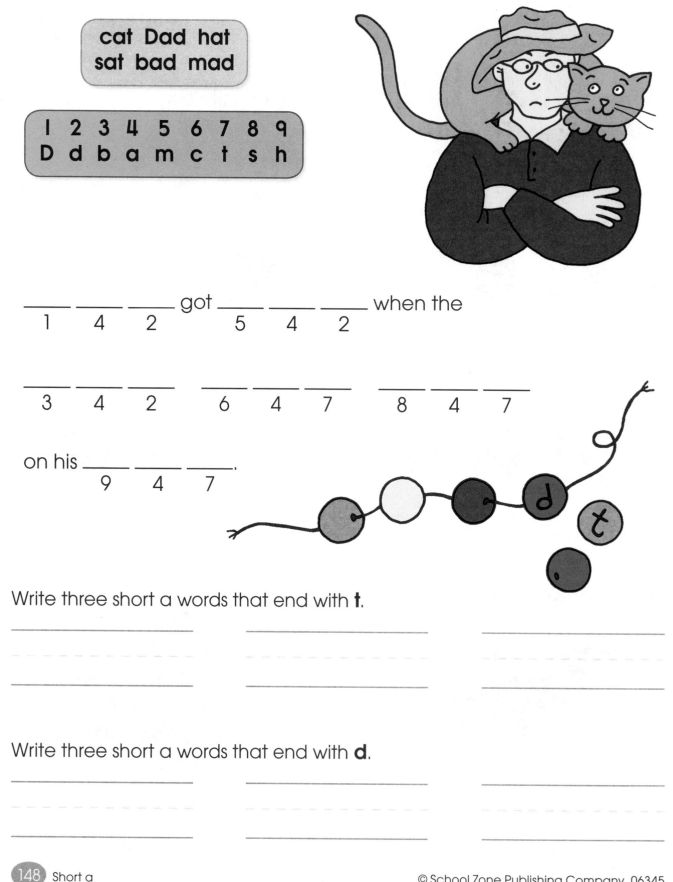

___ ___ ___ got ___ ___ ___ when the
 1   4   2   5   4   2

___ ___ ___ ___ ___ ___ ___ ___ ___
 3   4   2   6   4   7   8   4   7

on his ___ ___ ___.
        9   4   7

Write three short a words that end with **t**.

_____ _____ _____

_____ _____ _____

Write three short a words that end with **d**.

_____ _____ _____

_____ _____ _____

Words With Short a

Look at the word box. Circle the short a words in the puzzle.

hat ant bat map
mask sack apple rabbit

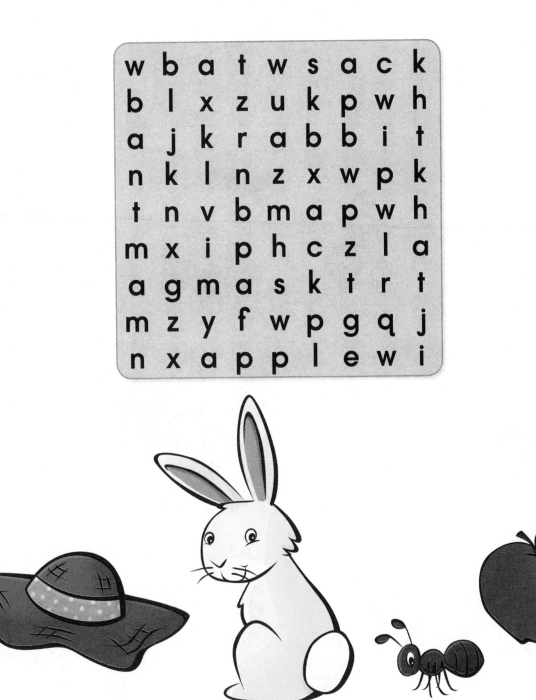

w b a t w s a c k
b l x z u k p w h
a j k r a b b i t
n k l n z x w p k
t n v b m a p w h
m x i p h c z l a
a g m a s k t r t
m z y f w p g q j
n x a p p l e w i

Words With Short e

Say each picture word.
Circle two **short e** pictures in each row.

short e sound
sled

Words With Short e

Write the short e word for each picture.

Short e 151

Words With Short e

Draw lines from the short e words to their pictures.
Then write the short e words under the pictures.

web

belt

pen

hen

desk

dress

Words With Short e

Look at the word box. Circle the short e words in the puzzle.

| egg bed sled cent |
| tent nest dress seven |

n t e n t k b e d
z p o m w b j l s
s k h w n e s t q
l n z x w o h d e
e n s e v e n j g
d m b t p w f l g
m x t p c e n t w
b t e l z v q l u
w d r e s s k n t

Words With Short i

Say each picture word.
Circle two **short i** pictures in each row.

Words With Short i

Write the short i word from the box that
rhymes with each picture word.

hit win fix
big crib dish

Words With Short i

Write the word that fits each shape.

six sit fish big
pig did give his

Write the word from the box that rhymes with each word below.

big _____

fix _____

live _____

hit _____

dish _____

hid _____

Words With Short i

Read the clues to finish the puzzle.

Across

2. The ____ fell and broke.
3. He gave the ball a hard ____.
4. A ____ is a very large boat.

Down

1. A ____ is a very young chicken.
3. I gave Mother a ____ goodbye.
5. A young hog is called a ____.

dish kick kiss
chick pig ship

Words With Short o

Say each picture word.
Circle two **short o** pictures in each row.

Words With Short o

Color the short o words in the picture orange.
Color the other words green.

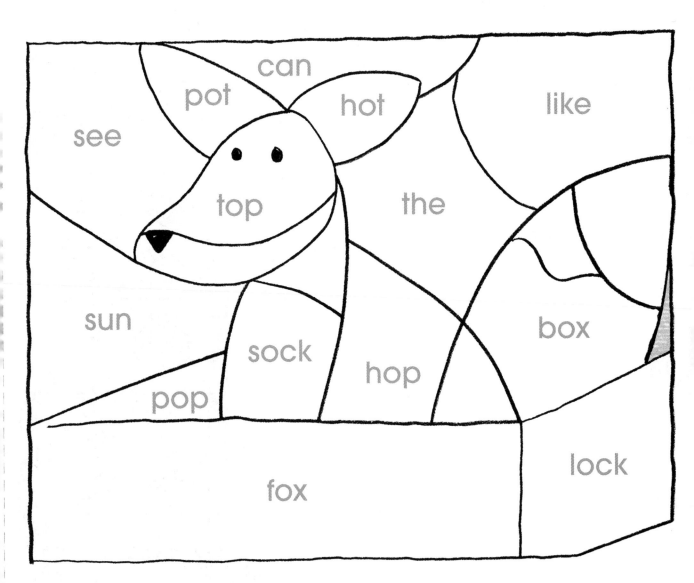

Finish the sentence with short o words from the puzzle.

_____   _____

The _____ is in the _____ .

Words With Short o

Write the word to finish each sentence.

> **pop top mom
> hot job hop**

The soup is too _____.

How far can you _____?

The balloon burst with a _____!

His _____ said he can go.

It is my _____ to set the table.

The book is on the _____ shelf.

Read the clues to finish the puzzle.

Across

clock sock lock
spot hot block

2. The pen made an ink ＿＿ on her dress.
4. The ＿＿ is five minutes fast.
5. Make sure you ＿＿ the door.

Down

1. The soup is too ＿＿ to eat.
2. I have a hole in my ＿＿.
3. My friend lives a ＿＿ away from me.

Words With Short u

Say each picture word.
Circle two **short u** pictures in each row.

short u sound
drum

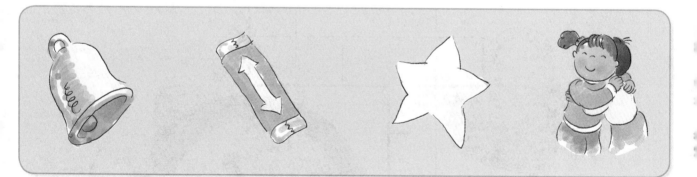

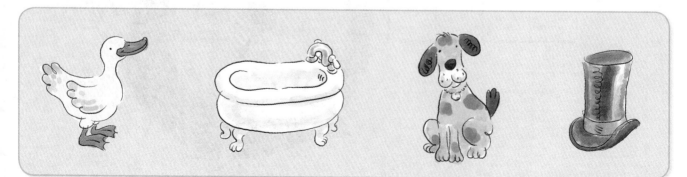

© School Zone Publishing Company 06345

Words With Short u

Draw a line connecting all the short u words.

Words With Short u

Write the short u word from the box that rhymes with each word below.
Then circle each word in the puzzle.

> nut up gum bug
> bus tub duck fun

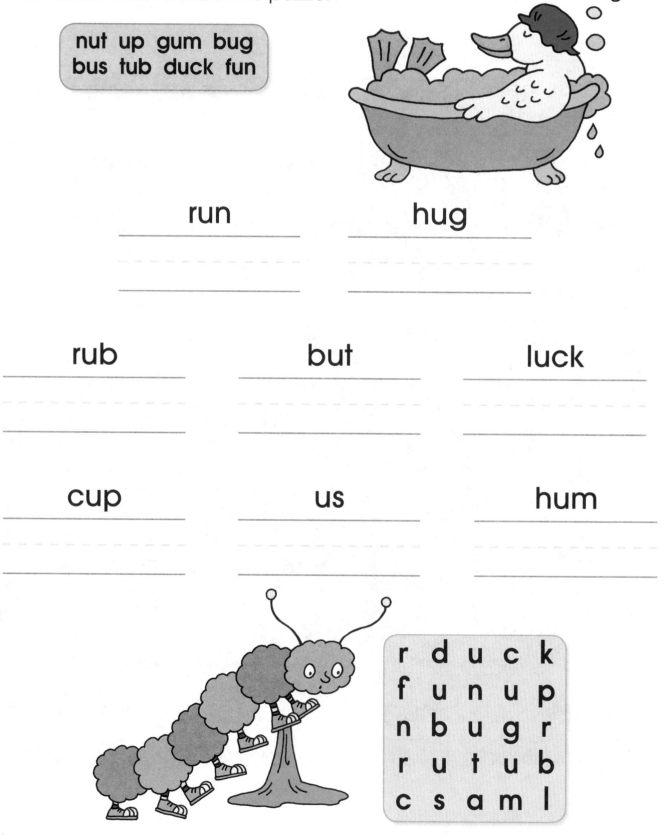

run

hug

rub

but

luck

cup

us

hum

r	d	u	c	k
f	u	n	u	p
n	b	u	g	r
r	u	t	u	b
c	s	a	m	l

Words With Short u

Read the clues to finish the puzzle.

Across

2. We saw a ____ swimming in the pond.
3. I had to ____ over the puddle.
5. Harry tells ____ jokes.

Down

1. A ____ can carry things too big for a car.
2. I play a ____ in the band.
4. A ____ is a young dog.

> truck jump drum
> puppy duck funny

Say each picture word.
Write the short vowel to
complete each picture word.

a e i o u
fox

t __ n

c __ t

p __ g

b __ s

d __ ll

f __ n

f __ sh

n __ st

d __ ck

Review Short Vowels

Say the name of each picture.
Circle the short vowel sound heard in each word.

a e i o u

a e i o u

a e i o u

a e i o u

a e i o u

Words With Long a

Write the **long a** words to answer each riddle.

rain gray cake
day gate snail

long a sound
snake

I live in a shell.

_____

I wear candles on your birthday.

_____

I make flowers grow.

_____

I am the opposite of night.

_____

Write two long a words that begin with **g**.

_____ _____

_____ _____

Words With Long a

Write the long a words to answer each riddle.

rake game tape
vase cake gate

You can put flowers in me.

_____

_____

I fix a torn page.

_____

_____

You use me to pile leaves.

_____

_____

You like to eat me.

_____

_____

Write two long a words that begin with **g**.

_____   _____

_____   _____

Words With Long a

Find three in a row like tic-tac-toe.
Draw lines through the long a words.

so	bow	cake
hat	cab	rake
look	hook	tape

are	toy	pan
play	day	say
cub	tie	an

hid	way	cap
mad	vase	hop
new	race	pet

pay	cup	ham
goat	may	cow
bat	cold	hay

Words With Long a

Write the long a words for the pictures.

| paint | rain | made | say | wait | cake | hay | train |

Words With Long e

Write the long e word to answer each riddle.

sheep leaf he
three tree me

long e sound
seal

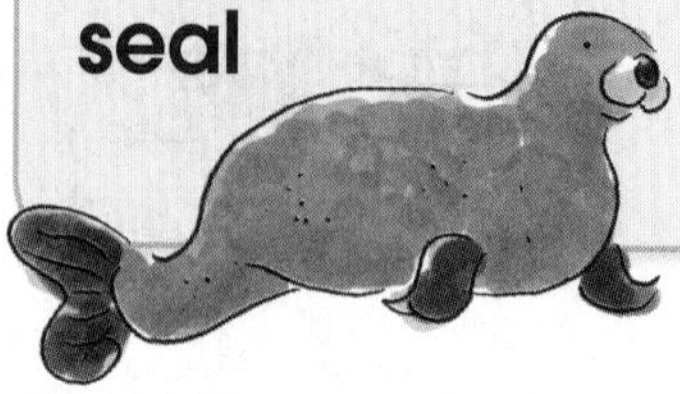

I come after two.

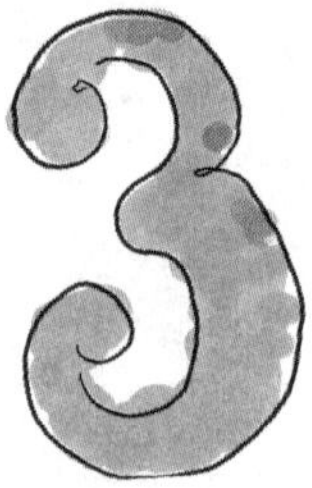

_____

_____

I grow outside.

_____

_____

I say "baa!"

_____

_____

I grow on a tree.

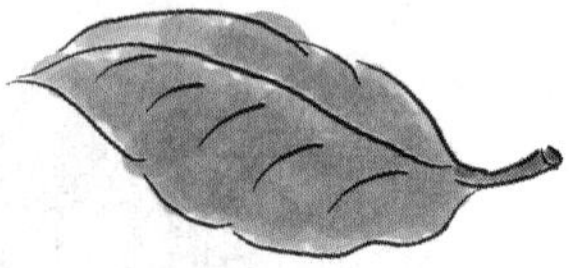

_____

_____

Write two long e words that end with **e**.

_____   _____

_____   _____

Words With Long e

he me see
three she tree

Write the 2-letter long e words that rhyme with **bee**.

_____   _____

_____   _____

Write the 3-letter long e words that rhyme with **bee**.

_____   _____

_____   _____

Write the long e words for the pictures.

_____   _____

_____   _____

Words With Long e

Write the long e word to answer each riddle.

Me? He!

bee seal me
tree he leaf

I can swim.

_____

I am a large plant.

_____

I can change color in the fall.

_____

I get food from flowers.

_____

Write the 2-letter long e words.

_____   _____

Words With Long e

Read the clues.
Write the long e answers in the puzzle.

see bean key
clean leave seed
money dream tree

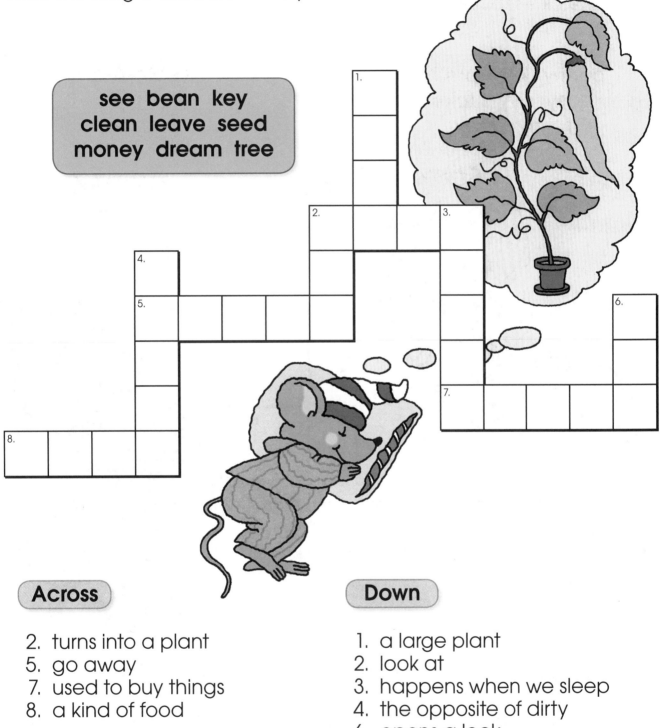

Across

2. turns into a plant
5. go away
7. used to buy things
8. a kind of food

Down

1. a large plant
2. look at
3. happens when we sleep
4. the opposite of dirty
6. opens a lock

Words Ending With y

Y has a long e sound at the end of some words.

Read the clues to finish the puzzle.

penny kitty pretty
easy silly lucky
funny baby

Across

3. causing laughter
5. not hard
7. foolish
8. very young child

Down

1. cute
2. having good luck
4. one cent
6. baby cat

Words With Long i

Write the **long i** word to answer each riddle.

> fly right tie
> bike tight nine

long i sound
kite

You can ride me.

_____

_____

I come before ten.

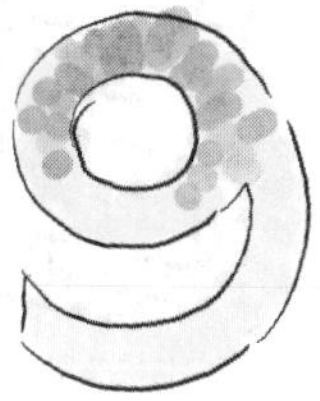

_____

_____

A plane can do this.

_____

_____

This is the opposite of left.

_____

_____

Write two long i words that begin with **t**.

_____   _____

_____   _____

Words With Long i

Write the long i words for the pictures.

| dime | kite | write | time | tire | bike | fire | hive |

Words With Long i

Read the clues.
Write the long i answers in the puzzle.

Across

2. My answer is _____.
3. My _____ has a horn.

Down

1. My _____ flies high.
2. I can _____ my new bike.

light right
kite bike ride

Write a long i word to finish the sentence.
_____

Please turn on the _____.

Words With Long i

Write the long i words to finish the sentences.

| hide | tire | size | die | shy | cry | like | line |

Our car has a flat _____.

The boys are the same _____.

I heard the baby _____ for her mother.

Maisy looks _____ her mom.

We waited in _____ for the bus.

A deer is a _____ animal.

A plant will _____ without water.

We like to _____ Easter eggs.

Words With Long o

Write the **long o** word to answer each riddle.

rose goat rope
nose boat note

long o sound
coat

I live on a farm.

_____

_____

You can tie things with me.

_____

_____

I move in water.

_____

_____

I am a kind of flower.

_____

_____

Write two long o words that begin with **n**.

_____   _____

_____   _____

Words With Long o

Circle these long o words in the puzzle.
Look across and down.

note hope fold
gold home told

z	h	o	m	e	u	g	n
y	o	r	p	o	b	o	m
h	x	d	v	t	o	l	d
o	e	w	y	x	r	d	e
p	r	n	o	t	e	y	a
e	a	u	f	s	a	v	c
m	u	l	d	f	o	l	d

Dear Ed,
See you Thursday!
From,
Michael

Words With Long o

Write the long o words for the pictures.

hole rose rope bone notes mole pole home

Words With Long o

Write the long o words to finish the sentences.

| show   low   road   grow   snow   goat   slow   coat |

_____

Will it _____ today?

_____

The _____ is bumpy.

_____

My _____ keeps me warm.

_____

It jumped over a _____ wall.

_____

Will you _____ me how it works?

_____

The clock is _____.

_____

Did the _____ eat the apple?

_____

The tree will _____ very high.

© School Zone Publishing Company 06345

Words With Long o Sound: o, oa, ow

Write the word for each clue.
Then read the letters in the box to answer the riddle.

own	told	show	both	coat	grow	goat

get bigger ___ ___ ___ ___

worn over clothes ___ ___ ___ ___

put in sight ___ ___ ___ ___

one, then another ___ ___ ___ ___

have ___ ___ ___

a farm animal ___ ___ ___ ___

said; put into words ___ ___ ___ ___

I float on water.

What am I? _____

Add the missing letters to make words.

gr ___ ___   sh ___ ___   ___ wn   t ___ ld

c ___ ___ t   b ___ th   g ___ ___ t

Words With Long u

Write the **long u** word to answer each riddle.

cute tube new
huge few glue

long u sound
cube

Toothpaste comes in a _____.

_____

_____

Use me to stick things together.

_____

_____

A whale is _____.

_____

_____

Babies are _____.

_____

_____

Write two long u words that are spelled with **ew**.

_____   _____

_____   _____

Words With Long u

Write the long u words to finish the sentences.

| true | few | cute | huge | view | use |

If there aren't many, there are _____.

If it is not false, it is _____.

I thought the baby was very _____.

An elephant is a _____ animal.

Standing on a mountain, you have a nice _____.

When you work with something, you _____ it.

Words With Long u

Use the code to write the long u words.

mule tube true
cube use ruler

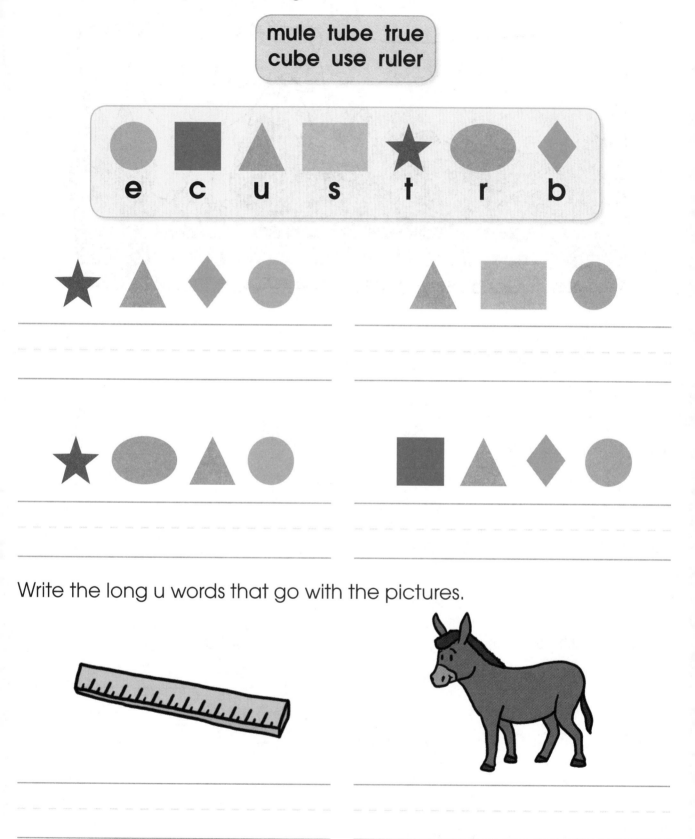

Write the long u words that go with the pictures.

© School Zone Publishing Company 06345

Words With Long u

Write the long u words to finish the sentences.

huge	use	cute	cube	ruler	mule

_____

The baby is _____.

_____

An elephant is _____.

_____

A _____ looks like a horse.

_____

Put an ice _____ in my drink.

_____

A _____ has 12 inches.

_____

You can _____ this book to learn words!

Vowel-Consonant-e

Many words with a long vowel sound are spelled with vowel-consonant-**e** (mad - made).

Add an **e** to each word to make a new word.

at ____   kit ____   pin ____

hug ____   dim ____   mad ____

Help fly the kites.
Write each word from above on the correct kite.

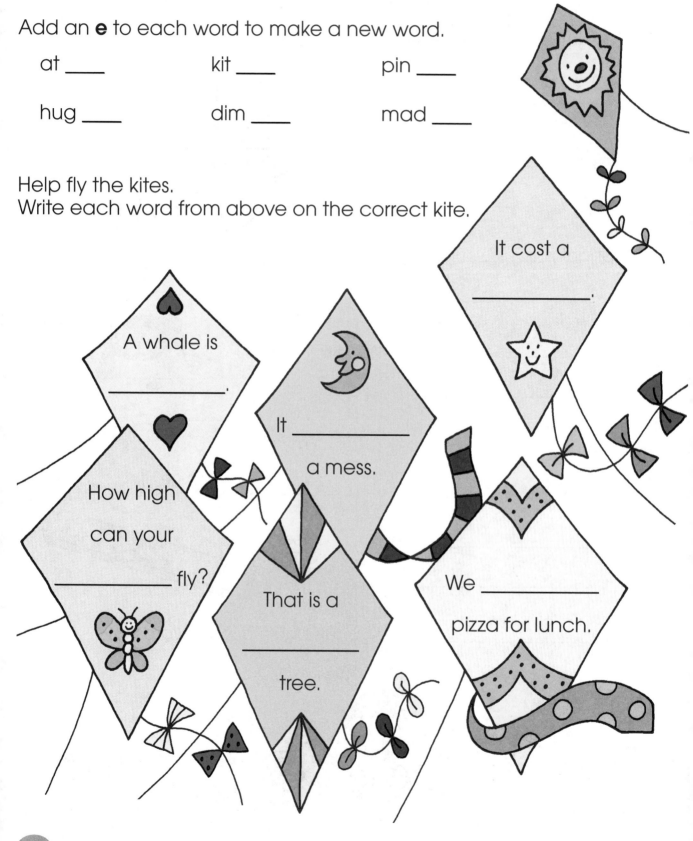

It cost a

_____.

A whale is

_____.

It _____

a mess.

How high

can your

_____ fly?

That is a

_____

tree.

We _____

pizza for lunch.

Vowel-Consonant-e

Write the word for each clue.
Then read the letters in the box to answer the riddle.

> home dime pine those
> nine cute save make

keep ___ ___ ___ ___

pretty ___ ___ ___ ___

one more than eight ___ ___ ___ ___

plural of that ___ ___ ___ ___ ___

where a person lives ___ ___ ___ ___

a 10¢ coin ___ ___ ___ ___

a kind of tree ___ ___ ___ ___

build ___ ___ ___ ___

_____

I brighten your day. What am I? _____

Add the missing letters to make words.

c ___ t ___   s ___ v ___   h ___ m ___   m ___ k ___

d ___ m ___   th ___ s ___   n ___ n ___   p ___ n ___

Draw a line from each picture to the long vowel sound in its name.

long a

long e

long i

long o

long u

Playtime Puzzles

Look at the pictures. Say the words.
Write the missing long vowels in the puzzle.

Across

1.

4.

6.

Down

2.

3.

5.

1. r		2. k	e		3. b
		4. t		5. b	e
		e			
				n	
6. s	l		d	e	

Review: Long Vowels

Write the long vowel words to finish the sentences.

same   jeans   know   **money**   time   snails   coat   **cube**

A clock tells _____.

I _____ the answer.

We have the _____ first name.

My dirty _____ need to be washed.

Wear your warmest _____ today.

A _____ has six sides.

_____ move very slowly.

How much _____ does the ticket cost?

© School Zone Publishing Company 06345

Sentences

A **sentence** is a group of words that tells a complete thought. Every sentence begins with an uppercase letter and ends with an end mark.

I like to go to the pond.
This is a sentence.

my friends bring
This is not a sentence.

Read each group of words.
Write **yes** if the words make a sentence.
Write **no** if they do not.

We are going to the pond. _____

frogs and log. _____

I saw a bird. _____

It flew to a tree. _____

have wings and feathers. _____

Write a sentence.

_____

_____

_____

_____

Backyard Barbeque

A sentence has a **telling part**.
The telling part tells what someone or something does.

Underline the telling part of each sentence.
The first one is done for you.

Dani <u>brings milk</u>.

Josh has bananas.

Wen takes a salad.

Billy carries hot dogs.

They all eat together.

Write a sentence about a picnic.
Underline the telling part.

_____

_____

_____

Who didn't bring anything? _____

Animals at the Fair

Fill in the missing naming word to complete each sentence.
Use the words in the box.

pig horse dog
duck cow goat

The _____ is tall.

The _____ is fat!

The _____ has horns.

The spotted _____ moos.

The _____ eats corn.

Is the _____ lost?

Mystery Bus

Read the picture story.

Amy got on the bus.

It was her first bus ride ever.

The driver showed Amy her seat.

The bus stopped many times.

Other kids got on.

Where was the bus going?

Circle the correct answers.

What did Amy get on?	bus	boat
Who showed Amy where to sit?	mother	driver
Who got on when the bus stopped?	dogs	kids
Did Amy ride the bus before?	yes	no
Did the bus stop a lot?	yes	no

Answer the question.

Where was the bus going?

_____

_____

Fish Story

Read the story.

> Cookie is a cat.
> Cookie likes to cook.
> Cookie cooks cake.
> He cooks it from fish.
> Cookie cooks pie from fish, too.
> Cookie even cooks cookies from fish!

Circle the correct answers.

What is the best name for the story?

A Real Cat   A Cat That Cooks

What does Cookie use to make everything he cooks?

fish   cake

What kind of animal is Cookie?

a real cat   a make-believe cat

Which sentences are correct? Circle **yes** or **no**.

Real cats can cook.   yes   no

Real cats can eat fish.   yes   no

Cookie is a real cat.   yes   no

Birthday Invitation

Read the invitation.

Come to a party!

What:
Jenny's birthday party

Where:
Jenny's house

Date:
May 5

Time:
2:00 p.m.

Circle the correct answers.

Who is having the party?	Jenny	birthday
What is the party for?	birthday	house
Where will the party be?	park	house
What day is the party?	May 5	2:00 p.m.
What time is the party?	2:00 p.m.	May 5

Answer the question.

What will you take to the party?

_____

I will take _____

_____

_____

Thank You

Read.

> Dear Grandma,
> You sent such a nice surprise!
> Thank you for my new skates.
> They will look great with my new helmet.
>
> I love you,
> Maria

Circle the correct answers.

What kind of writing is this?

a note   a birthday card

Who wrote it?

Maria   Grandma

Who is it for?

Grandma   Maria

What will Maria wear with her skates?

Jump Rope Rhyme

Read the poem.

> A-B-C-D-E-F-G
> Letters make the words I see.
>
> H-I-J-K Yes, indeed!
> I love letters. Can't you see?
>
> Skip, jump. L-M-N-O-P
> Q-R-S and T-U-V
>
> W and X and Y and Z
> ABCs are fun for me!

Circle the correct answers.

What is the poem about?

    seeing the sun   the alphabet

What is another good name for the poem?

Letter Fun   Happy Birthday

What makes the words we see?

  letters   me

What is the alphabet for me?

  easy   fun

Baseball Cheer

Read the poem.

> Our team is the best.
> Our team never rests.
>
> Our team really hits.
> Our team never quits.
>
> Before the games begin,
> We know that we will win!

Circle the correct answers.

What is the poem about?

our baseball team   our school

What is a team?

a group that works together   a person who works

Which word finishes the sentence?
"Our team never ____."

quits   loses

Which word rhymes with **quits**?

hits   rests

A Guessing Game

Read.

> You see me at the beach.
> You see me in a game.
> I am round and filled with air.
> I can be many colors.
> What am I?

Circle the correct answers.

What kind of writing is this?

a note   a riddle

What is the best name for the riddle?

What Am I?   Games and Work

What is the riddle about?

a beach ball   a float

Which sentences are correct?
Circle **yes** or **no**.

It is filled with air.   yes   no

It is always red.   yes   no

It is round.   yes   no

Dear Mom

Read.

Mom,
I am outside. I went to the park. Adam is with me. We will be home by noon.

I love you,
Erica

Circle the correct answers.

What kind of writing is this?

a sign   a note

Did Mom write the note?   yes   no

Is this note to Adam?   yes   no

Is Erica going to the park?   yes   no

Will Erica be home by noon?   yes   no

Who do you think Adam is?

Erica's friend   Erica's teacher

Leaves

Read the story.

> The wind was blowing.
> Leaves fell from the trees.
> Many leaves were red,
> orange, and yellow.
> Ty found a red leaf.
> Which season was it?

Circle the correct answers.

What is another good name for the story?

Winter   The Red Leaf

Which picture shows the weather that day?

What did Ty find?

Which season was it?

spring   summer   fall   winter

Mouse's House

Read the story.

> Mouse needed a house.
> It did not have to be big or pretty.
> It had to be dry and warm because winter was coming.
>
> Mouse looked in a tree.
> It was not warm.
> Mouse looked under a leaf.
> It was not dry.
> Mouse found a boot.
> It was dry and warm.
> Mouse had a new home.

Circle the correct answers.

What is the story about?

    finding a house   Mouse's family

What did the house have to be?

    warm and dry   big and dry

Why did Mouse need a house?

    He was lost.   Winter was coming.

Which is Mouse's new house?

Wish You Were Here!

Read each postcard. Draw lines to match the cards with the friends who wrote them. Write the name(s) on each card.

Hi,
We are having a great time camping. We saw deer and a bear yesterday. Wish you were here.

_____

_____

_____

Howdy,
This ranch is lots of fun. I ride a horse named Sugarlump. I learned to rope a calf. There is a cookout tonight.

_____

_____

Write words from the box to answer the questions.

> **ocean   calf   bear   horse   desert**

_____

Dani and Josh saw what animal? _____

_____

Where did Wen swim? _____

Hi,
The desert is neat. One cactus is taller than my house! I heard a coyote last night. See you soon.

_____

_____

Hi,
The ocean is great! I swim every day. I have made three sandcastles. Wish you were here to look for seashells with me.

_____

_____

SUGARLUMP

What animal did Pedro rope? _____

Who is Sugarlump? _____

Where does a cactus grow? _____

Capitalization & Punctuation

As you've learned, a sentence begins with a capital letter and ends with an end mark.

Butterflies like sunshine.

Use the proofreader's mark to correct mistakes.

≡	Make a capital.
⊙	Add a period.

a butterfly begins life as an egg.
≡   ⊙

Butterflies are insects

there are many kinds of butterflies.

butterflies live all over the world.

they help flowers become fruit and seeds

Most butterflies fly during the day

Postcards from Camp

Some children wrote postcards from camp. They forgot to use a capital letter to begin the name of a person, a pet, or a month. Find and circle each word that needs a capital letter.

Dear Mom,

Please pat my dog pat and say hello to him for me.

Love, Tim

Dear Dad,

A lucky girl named penny found a penny in the woods.

Love, Katie

Dear Grandma,

My best friend may come and visit me in may.

Love, Jon

Dear Kelly,

Next march, people from my camp will march in a parade.

Love, Carrie

Dear Aunt Sue,

The camp's dog freckles has spots that look like freckles.

Love, Chuckie

Dino-Myte!

A **telling sentence** ends with a period (**.**).
An **asking sentence** ends with a question mark (**?**).

Put **.** or **?** at the end of each sentence.

Do you like dinosaurs ☐

Two dinosaurs are running ☐

Can some dinosaurs swim ☐

The big dinosaur is green ☐

Some dinosaurs eat plants ☐

How many spots does the small dinosaur have ☐

Naming Parts

A **naming part** of a sentence tells who or what the sentence is about.

My family planted a garden.
The backyard was a good place for a garden.

Underline the naming part in each sentence.
Then circle **who** or **what**.

Dad planted seeds.   who   what

The seeds began to grow.   who   what

My sisters watered them each day.   who   what

The plants grew big.   who   what

Flowers began to bloom.   who   what

The garden is pretty.   who   what

Write a naming part to complete each sentence.

_____

_____ is fun to visit.

_____

_____ and I go there often.

Telling Parts

The **telling part** of a sentence tells what someone or something is or does.

    People **shop for food**.
    The store **is crowded**.

Underline the telling part of each sentence.

Erica walks in the park.

She sees a rabbit.

The rabbit eats grass.

It looks at Erica.

It wiggles its nose.

Then the rabbit hops away.

Write a sentence. Underline the telling part.

_____

_____

_____

Exclamations & Statements

An **exclamation** is a sentence that shows strong feelings.
An exclamation begins with a capital letter and ends with
an exclamation point (**!**).
  Wow, the most amazing thing happened**!**
  Three cheers for the champs**!**

A **statement** is a sentence that tells something. A statement begins
with a capital letter and ends with a period (**.**)
  My cat had kittens**.**

Write an **!** after the exclamations.
Write a **.** after the statements.

I went to my friend's house ☐

He has a pet turtle ☐

Yikes, it bit my finger ☐

His mother gave us a snack ☐

Oops, the milk spilled ☐

Oh, no ☐

Questions

A **question** is a sentence that asks something. A question begins with a capital letter and ends with a question mark (**?**).

What do you want for lunch**?**

Do you like soup**?**

Most questions begin with a question word, such as **who**, **what**, **when**, **where**, **why**, **which**, or **how**.

Write a question word to begin each question.

How	Can	What	Who	Do

_____ you like pizza?

_____ we have pizza for dinner?

_____ do you like on your pizza?

_____ ate the piece of pizza?

_____ many pieces did you eat?

Write a question about food.

_____

Write a statement that answers your question.

_____

Question Words

Read the riddles. Write the answers.

Please come to a party!
WHO ___Alyssa___
WHEN ___Friday, Feb. 14___
WHY ___Valentine's Day___
WHERE ___121 Jones St.___
___(my house)___

| when | why | which | where | who |

_____

I ask for a name. _____

I ask for a place. _____

I ask for time. _____

I ask for a reason. _____

I ask for a choice. _____

Write a sentence that asks **what**.

_____

_____

_____

Soccer Practice

Read the story.

Sam and Pam were playing soccer on a soccer field. Pam asked Sam, "Do you want the ball?" Sam replied, "Yes, pass it to me!" Pam passed the ball to Sam. Sam was about to make a goal when he tripped and fell. Pam ran over to Sam. "Are you okay?"asked Pam. "I'm fine. I need to tie my shoelaces," whispered Sam. Pam helped Sam get back on his feet. "Let's try again," said Pam.

Write your answer with a sentence.

Who are the characters in the story?

_____

_____

What is the setting?

_____

_____

Why did Sam fall?

_____

_____

Apples Everywhere

Read the story.

> There are many kinds of apples.
> Apples are red, green, and yellow.
> All apples grow on trees.
> Some apples are sweet.
> Sweet apples taste good raw.
> Other apples are tart.
> Tart apples taste best cooked.

Circle the correct answers.

What is the story about?

    sweet things   apples

What colors are apples?

    red, green, yellow   red, blue, yellow

What does **tart** mean?

    sweet   sour

Which apples taste better cooked?

    tart apples   red apples

Which kinds of apples have you eaten?
Circle each kind you have tried.

Peanut Butter

Read the story.

You can eat peanut butter on bread. You can eat it on crackers. You can eat it with jam. I like to eat it on apples.

Peanut butter is made from peanuts and oil. The peanuts are ground up. Then you add a little oil. Now you have peanut butter.

Answer the questions.

What can we eat with peanut butter?

_____   _____

_____   _____

_____   _____

_____   _____

What is peanut butter made from?

_____   _____

_____ and _____

Do you like to eat peanut butter?

_____

_____

All About Dogs

Read the story.

In Alaska, dogs pull sleds over the snow. Dogsleds are better than cars in deep snow.

Dogs also help people who cannot see. The dogs lead the way and help the owners know where to go.

Have you seen a working dog?

Circle the correct answers.

What is the story about?

pet dogs   working dogs

What work do some dogs do?

drive cars   pull sleds

What other work do some dogs do?

help people who cannot see   help people sleep

Do dogs pull sleds?   yes   no

Do dogs drive cars?   yes   no

Do dogs help people?   yes   no

Giraffe Story

Read the story.

Giraffe likes to draw and dance. She thought she should do just one. Giraffe got dancing shoes. She danced every day.

Giraffe went to the tryout for the dance group, but she was too tall for the stage!

At first, Giraffe was sad. Then she had a good idea! She would draw dancers. Then she would be part of both things she likes!

Circle the correct answers.

Did Giraffe want to be a dancer?   yes   no

Did Giraffe get dancing shoes?   yes   no

Did Giraffe go to Dancing School?   yes   no

What do you find out at a tryout?

if you can join   if you are too smart

What is a good name for the story?

Drawing   Dancing   Giraffe's Idea

Unscramble the words to answer the question.

What was Giraffe's good idea?   **dwra dcreans**

_____

Giraffe would _____

Surprise Sunday

Read the story.

> When Zach woke up, no one was home. Where was his family? Zach heard a barking sound. What was it?
>
> Zach found his family in the backyard. "Happy Birthday!" they said. They were playing with Zach's new puppy.

Circle the correct answers.

What is the best name for the story?

    Zach's Surprise   The Family Car

What did Zach hear?

    a laugh   a sound

Draw lines to match the parts of the sentences.

When Zach woke up,   no one was home.

"Happy Birthday!"   with Zach's new puppy.

They were playing   they said.

The Dance

Read the story.

It would be the best dance!
Every dinosaur was coming.
Deeny wanted to be cool.
He got out his cool dino shoes.

Uh-oh! One shoe has a hole.
Deeny filled the hole with gum.
When the music began,
Deeny stuck to the floor!
Deeny took off his shoes.
He was cool anyway.

Circle the correct answers.

What is another good name for the story?

Real Dinosaurs   Deeny's Dino Shoes

What did Deeny put in his shoe?

gum   a hole

What happened then?

Deeny stuck to the floor.   Deeny fell down.

Which one is Deeny?

The Alien

Read the story.

> Hal did not like being an alien.
> He wanted to be a kid.
> He left his planet.
> He went to Earth.
>
> Hal saw a doll.
> He thought it was a kid.
> The doll did not talk.
> It was not fun, so Hal
> went back home.

Circle the correct answers.

What is the story about?

    a doll   an alien

What is an **alien**?

    someone from another planet

    a kid who wants to be a doll

What did Hal want to be?

    a doll   a kid

Which one is Hal?

Monster Fun

Read the story.

> The monsters had a party.
> They played monster games.
> They did monster dances.
> Then they cleaned up.
>
> Monster Mom said, "Monsters
> are messy. Mess this room up,
> right now!"

Circle the correct answers.

Which one is a monster?

What is another good name for the story?

A Monster Party   Monster Foods

What did Monster Mom want the monsters to do?

clean up   make a mess

Draw lines to match the words that are opposites.

clean   worked

played   messy

Living in a Boot

Read the story.

> There was an old woman who lived in a boot. She fed all her children crackers and fruit.
>
> When nighttime would come, she'd say, "Off to bed! Scoot!" And she'd play them to sleep with a song from her flute.

Circle the correct answers.

What is the poem about?

    boots   an ant family

What does **scoot** mean?

    go quickly   go slowly

What does the woman make with her flute?

    boots   music

Which pictures have names that rhyme with scoot?

The Bug

Read the story.

> Willie was a little car.
> Everyone called him "The Bug."
> Willie couldn't go fast, but he was always ready.
>
> One day, the family had a problem.
> They got in their fast car, but it didn't go.
>
> Willie was ready. Willie saved the day!

Circle the correct answers.

What is the story about?

a family   a car

What is the best name for the story?

Fast Cars Are Best   Willie Saves the Day

What was it that Willie could not do?

go slow   go fast

Which one is Willie?

Scary Night

Read the story.

> The night was dark.
> Tina heard something go "whooo!"
> Tina was scared.
>
> The window blew open.
> Tina saw an owl.
> The owl went "whooo!"
> Tina was not scared then.

Circle the correct answers.

What is the story about?

how owls live   a scary night

What is the best name for the story?

A Scary Sound   Tina's Pet

What did Tina hear?

a ghost   an owl

Number the sentences from **1** to **4** to show the correct order.

☐ The window blew open.   ☐ Tina was scared.

☐ Tina saw an owl.   ☐ Tina was not scared then.

Monkey Poem

Read the poem.

> Five little monkeys went to play
> out in the park one sunny day.
>
> When Uncle Baboon said,
> "On your way!"
> All the little monkeys said,
> "Can we stay?"
>
> Uncle Baboon said, "Oh, okay!
> I do like to see my monkeys play."

Circle the correct answers.

What is a good name for the poem?

    Monkeys in the Park   The Mad Baboon

Who was the baboon?

    the monkeys' dad   the monkeys' uncle

Was only one monkey playing?   yes   no

Did the monkeys want to stay?   yes   no

Did the baboon let them stay?   yes   no

Read the story.

> A stranger walked into the barn.
> He was wearing a long coat and a hat.
> He had hair on his chin. He did not talk.
> Who was he?
>
> Cow was afraid. Horse was afraid.
> Rat went to take a closer look.
> The stranger's legs were hairy.
> He had a tail. It was just Goat.
> Goat was playing a trick!

Circle the correct answers.

What is the best name for the story?

The Animals   Stranger in the Barn

What did the stranger wear?

a hat and pants   a hat and a coat

Who was wearing the coat?

Horse   Goat

What was Goat doing?

playing a trick   trying to hide

School Mystery

Read the story.

> Jess got dressed.
> She ate her breakfast.
> She kissed her mom and
> walked to school.
>
> No one was there!
> The rooms were empty.
> The doors were locked.
> "Oh, no! It's Saturday!" Jess said.

Circle the correct answers.

What is the best name for the story?

Jess Goes to School   Go to the Store

What day was it?

Monday   Saturday

Where did Jess go?

to school   to the park

How did Jess get there?

The Artist

Read the story.

Pete is an artist, but everything Pete draws looks like Pete.

Pete painted a house. It was big, tan, and furry. Pete painted the door. It had sharp teeth. Pete painted a garden. The flowers looked like claws. Silly Pete!

Circle the correct answers.

What is the best name for the story?

Pete's Garden   Pete, the Artist

Is Pete a person?   yes   no

Is Pete a bear?   yes   no

Does Pete have claws?   yes   no

Draw a picture that Pete might draw.

Kids at Work

Read the story.

> Kids can do many jobs.
> They can rake leaves.
> They can sweep sidewalks.
> They can help carry packages.
>
> Kids are not ready to do some jobs.
> They cannot drive buses.
> They cannot drive dump trucks.

Circle the correct answers.

What is the best name for the story?

Jobs for Kids　　　Kids Are Too Little

What is a job that kids can do?

drive buses　　　sweep sidewalks

What is a job that kids cannot do?

rake leaves　　　drive cars

Answer the question.

What work will you do when you grow up?

_____

_____

_____

Our Flag

Read the story.

This is our American flag.
Some people call our flag
"The Stars and Stripes."
Our flag is red, white, and blue.
The flag has 13 stripes.
Seven are red. Six are white.
There are 50 stars. There is one
star for each state in our country.

Circle the correct answers.

What is the story about?

the American flag   stripes

What color are the stripes?

red and blue   red and white

How many red stripes are there?
How many white stripes are there?

50 red, 13 white   7 red, 6 white

Answer the question.

Why are there 50 stars?

_____

_____

_____

_____

Book Cover

Read about book covers.

> A book cover tells the name of a book.
> It tells who wrote the book.
> It tells who drew the pictures.

MY VALENTINE BOOK
Written by Tyrone James
Pictures by Robert James

Check the things that a book cover tells.

☐ who wrote the book

☐ when the book was made

☐ the name of the book

☐ who drew the pictures

Answer the questions about the cover shown on this page.

Who wrote this book?

_____

_____

Who drew the pictures?

_____

_____

What is this book about?

_____

_____

Slippery Slide

Read the rhyme.
Then draw a line under each number word.

Penguin Pals

Five little penguin pals resting on the shore.

One took a dip, and then there were four.

Four little penguin pals walking by the sea.

One little slip, and then there were three.

Three little penguin pals with nothing to do.

One little trip, and then there were two.

Two little penguin pals looking for fun.

One little flip, and then there was one.

One little penguin all alone.

He jumped in too, and now there are none.

Write the words that rhyme with **tip**.
Say other words that rhyme with **tip**.

Reading Comprehension 237

Nouns name people, places, and things.

Help the family get home.
Draw a line connecting all of the words
that name people.

girl

kite

boy

tree

car

father

mother

house

baby

Words That Name Places

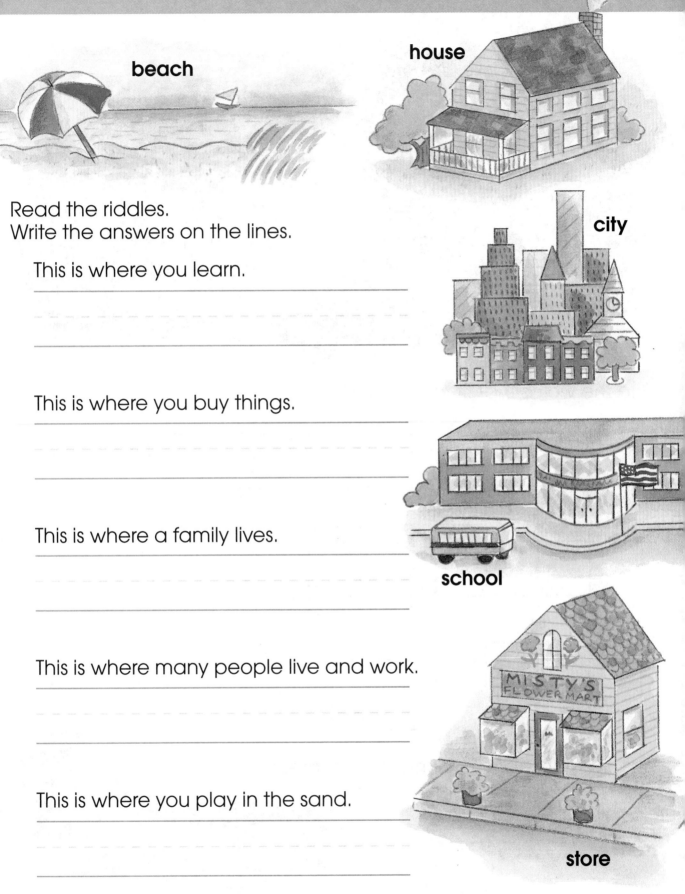

beach

house

city

Read the riddles.
Write the answers on the lines.

This is where you learn.

_____

This is where you buy things.

_____

This is where a family lives.

_____

school

This is where many people live and work.

_____

This is where you play in the sand.

_____

store

Words That Name Animals

Write the words that fit the shapes.

Write the name of an animal that rhymes with **cat**.

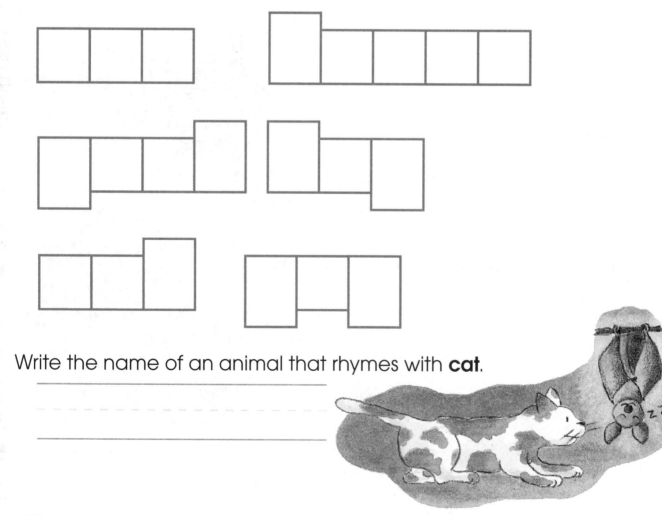

Words That Name Things

Find three in a row like tic-tac-toe.
Draw lines through the words that name things.

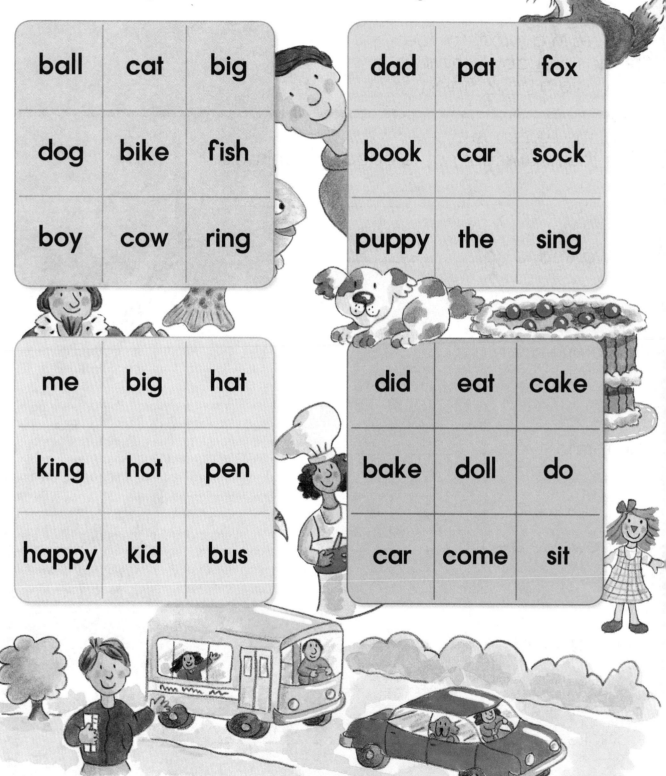

ball	cat	big
dog	bike	fish
boy	cow	ring

dad	pat	fox
book	car	sock
puppy	the	sing

me	big	hat
king	hot	pen
happy	kid	bus

did	eat	cake
bake	doll	do
car	come	sit

Nouns

The underlined words in these sentences are nouns.
Nouns name people, places, or things.

We are going to visit my <u>aunt</u>. (person)
She lives in a <u>forest</u>. (place)
She has a <u>puppy</u>. (animal)
She wrote a <u>book</u>. (thing)

Read the sentences.
Write the nouns that name people or animals.

_____

Billy wanted to go. _____

_____

Dad drove away. _____

_____

The farmer waved. _____

_____

The cows were eating. _____

_____

Our dog barked. _____

_____

A chicken ran away. _____

Nouns

The underlined words in these sentences are nouns. Nouns name people or things.

My <u>uncle</u> sees a <u>whale</u>.
That <u>fish</u> is blue.
<u>Animals</u> are fun to watch.

Read the sentences. Underline the nouns.
Then write each noun under its picture.

The fish swim fast.

My brother feeds the dolphin.

The turtles are resting.

My aunt likes the penguins.

Nouns

The underlined words in these sentences are nouns.
Nouns name places or things.

Take the <u>rake</u> to the <u>barn</u>.
Paint the <u>fence</u>.
The <u>tractor</u> is ready.

Read the sentences. Underline the nouns.
Then write each noun in the chart.

The family has a busy farm.

The cows are being milked.

The hens are laying eggs.

A friend is painting the fence.

The horse waits in the barn.

My uncle is on his tractor.

People	Animals	Places	Things

Dog Days

Nouns name a person, place, or thing.
> sister   house   flower

Most nouns that name more than one end with **s**.
> sister**s**   house**s**   flower**s**

Finish each sentence.
Choose a word from the box.
Add **s** to make the word mean more than one.

> **bone   dog   cat   tail   pal**

I have two _____.

They bark at _____.

They wag their _____.

They chew on _____.

They are my _____.

Lots of Seeds

You add **s** to many nouns to make them name more than one.
Write these nouns in the sentences. Add **s**.

seed coconut dandelion tree

_____

Most plants grow from _____.

_____

The soft white fluff on _____ is their seeds.

_____

Some seeds become huge _____.

_____

Did you know that _____ are seeds?

You add **es** to nouns that end in **s**, **x**, **ch**, and **sh** to name
more than one. Write these nouns in the sentences. Add **es**.

wish teach class bus

_____

Green Gardens has _____ about plants.

_____

Students take _____ to the Gardens.

_____

My mother _____ she could come.

_____

She _____ at our school.

Use A and An

The words **a** and **an** are **articles**. Articles are used before nouns.

Use **a** before a word that begins with a consonant.
   A chicken sat on **a n**est.

Use **an** before a word that begins with a vowel or vowel sound.
   An ostrich laid **an e**gg.

Write **a** and **an** to complete each sentence.

_____   _____

If you give _____ elephant _____
peanut, she'll want peanut butter.

_____   _____

If you give _____ ant _____
crumb, he'll want a whole cake.

_____   _____

If you give _____ horse _____
apple, she'll want a bushel.

_____   _____

If you give _____ otter _____ fish,
he'll want a seafood platter.

_____   _____

If you give _____ fox _____ egg,
she'll want it scrambled.

Prefixes: un, mis

Un in front of a word means **not**.
Finish the word puzzle using the prefix **un**.
The first one is done for you.

u	n	h	a	p	p	y

not happy

not lucky

not clean

not clear

not fair

not seen

not tied

Mis in front of a word means **wrong**.
Finish the word puzzle using the prefix **mis**.

wrong count

wrong place

wrong lead

wrong match

wrong take

wrong use

Finish the word puzzle using the prefix **un**.

not afraid

not able

not safe

not kind

not even

not known

Finish the word puzzle using the prefix **mis**.

wrong fit

wrong step

wrong deal

wrong fire

wrong fortune

wrong spelling

Suffixes: ed, ing

Some words end with one **vowel** and one **consonant**.
To get the **short vowel** sound, double the final **consonant**
before adding **ed** or **ing**.

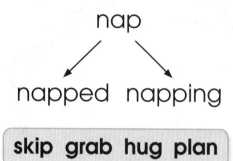

nap

napped   napping

skip   grab   hug   plan

Write the words using the **ed** ending.

_____   _____

_____   _____

_____   _____

_____   _____

Write the words using the **ing** ending.

_____   _____

_____   _____

_____   _____

_____   _____

Suffixes: ed, ing

Write the words with the correct endings to finish the sentences.

| skip | bat | hug | hop | sled | rub | grab | nap |

_____

The rabbit _____ into its hutch.

hop

_____

Jo _____ in the winning run.

bat

_____

A good exercise is _____ rope.

skip

_____

The baby is _____ in her crib.

nap

_____

I _____ the dish before it fell.

grab

_____

My bicycle tire is _____ against the fender.

rub

_____

The players _____ each other after the game.

hug

_____

The snow is perfect for _____ .

sled

Suffix: ing

If a word ends in **e**, drop the **e** and add **ing**.

like ———→ liking

Write the words with the correct endings to finish the sentences.

| make smile use race hide write come wash |

Sean is _____ a poem.
write

All of the runners were _____ to the finish line.
race

Raccoons like _____ their faces.
wash

Where was the cat _____ ?
hide

Dad is _____ a dollhouse for me.
make

The baby is _____ at the dog.
smile

We are _____ a strong soap to clean it.
use

Are you _____ to the party?
come

Suffix: es

If a word ends with a consonant and **y**, change the **y** to **i** and add **es**.

puppy ⟶ puppies

Write the words with the correct endings to finish the sentences.

| city   candy   lady   penny   berry   baby   story   cry |

My sister _____ when she can't come with me.
cry

Use your _____ to buy the gum.
penny

How many _____ have you visited?
city

The _____ are sleeping.
baby

My mother and I picked lots of _____.
berry

The chocolate factory makes lots of sweet _____.
candy

The _____ went shopping.
lady

Will you read us some more _____?
story

Suffixes Review

Nouns that end with **s, x, ch,** or **sh** add **es** to name more than one.

glass ⟶ glasses   bench ⟶ benches
fox ⟶ foxes   bush ⟶ bushes

Finish each silly sentence. Choose words from the word box.
Add **es** to make each word mean more than one.

| box   fox   lunch   bunch   peach   beach |

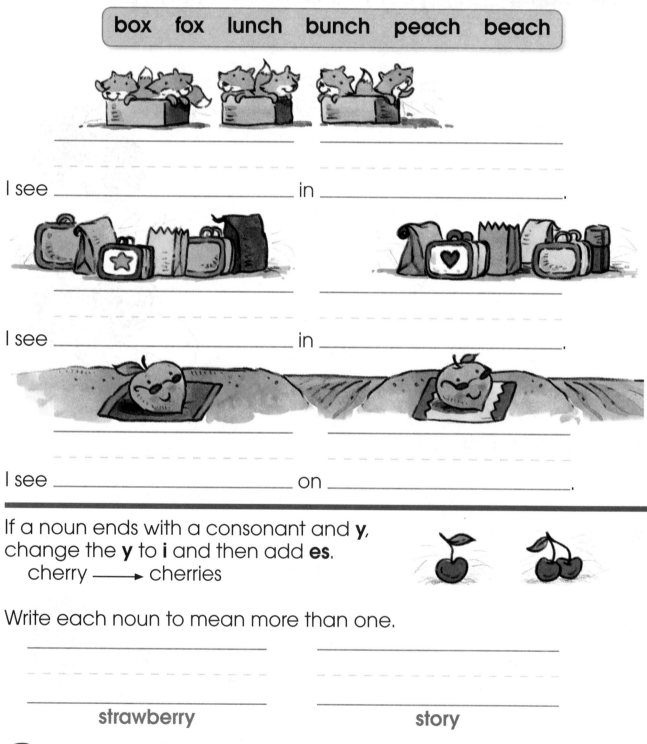

I see _____ in _____.

I see _____ in _____.

I see _____ on _____.

If a noun ends with a consonant and **y,**
change the **y** to **i** and then add **es.**

cherry ⟶ cherries

Write each noun to mean more than one.

_____   _____

_____   _____

strawberry   **story**

Plural means more than one.
Write the words with the correct endings.

Sometimes you add **s**.

book _____ clock _____

hand _____ flower _____

doll _____ mother _____

When the word ends in **ch**, **sh**, **ss**, or **x**, you add **es**.

box _____ pitch _____

dress _____ bench _____

wish _____ dish _____

When the word ends in **y**, you change the **y** to **i** and add **es**.

baby _____ cherry _____

pony _____ berry _____

city _____ penny _____

Proper Nouns

Special names of people, animals, and places are **proper nouns**. All proper nouns begin with a capital letter.

Find each pet's name in the word search. Then answer each clue with a pet's name.

A	P	E	T	E	R	H	J
F	D	A	X	Z	T	S	P
Q	V	V	G	H	P	L	O
B	U	B	B	L	E	S	L
H	F	X	Y	U	H	V	L
D	U	K	E	W	J	N	Y
A	S	Q	V	T	D	U	Q
D	P	U	F	F	M	K	L

_____

I can talk. _____

_____

I chase mice. _____

_____

I eat carrots. _____

_____

I live in water. _____

_____

I bark at strangers. _____

Where is Billy's House?

Texas
Colorado River
Austin

Riverside Drive

Billy lives in Austin, Texas.
He lives on Riverside Drive.
The Colorado River is near his house.

In which state does Billy live?
_____
- -
_____

In which city does Billy live?
_____
- -
_____

What is the name of his street?
_____
- -
_____

Which river is near Billy's house?
_____
- -
_____

Calendar Practice

Circle the name of the first day of the week.
Make a box around the name of the last day of the week.

May

Sunday	Monday	Tuesday	Wednesday	Thursday	Friday	Saturday
1	2	3	4	5 Pat's Birthday	6	7
8 Mother's Day	9	10	11	12	13	14

Which day is Mother's Day?

_____

_____

Which day is Pat's birthday?

_____

_____

What is the date of Pat's birthday?

_____

_____

Special Names

The special names of people, animals, and places are **proper nouns**. All proper nouns begin with a capital letter.

> **Aunt Alice** has a dog.
> Her dog is named **Tootsie**.

Correct the sentences by writing the mark ☰ under each letter that should be a capital. The first one is done for you.

aunt alice and tootsie are at the pet parade.

Tom came with his cat, muff.

Ben has his pig, petunia.

Last in line is grandpa jones.

He calls his silly goat, whiskers.

Write a sentence about someone's pet.

_____

_____

_____

_____

Days, Months, and Holidays

Some proper nouns name days, months, and holidays.
Thanksgiving is the last Thursday in November.

May   Saturday   Windmill Day

Choose proper nouns from the word box to complete the sentences.

In the country of Holland, children have a holiday
_____

called _____.
_____

It is celebrated in _____.
_____

It is on the second _____ of the month.

Write this mark ≡ under letters that should be capitalized in
the story.

I will spend july and august with my father. He lives in denver,

colorado. On independence day, we will visit the grand canyon. I

will be away until labor day. That is the first monday in september.

Write a sentence about your favorite holiday. Tell why you like it.
_____
_____

Special Places

Some proper nouns are names of special places.

Nouns	Proper Nouns
country	United States
state	Alaska
city	Fairbanks
street	Bell Lane
park	Yellowstone Park
forest	Pawnee Forest

Read the postcard. Find the names of special places.
Write this mark ≡ under letters that should be capitalized.

Dear Grandma,
    We are having so much
fun in arizona. Today, we went
to red rock canyon. The rocks
are so red. Tomorrow, we drive
to the tonto state forest. We will
camp there.   Love,
                      Chris

Mrs. Mary Morgan
28805 flower Street
roseville, michigan
                    48805

Write your address. Don't forget: The names of your street, city, and state are proper nouns.

_____

_____

_____

_____

Off to Camp!

A pronoun takes the place of a noun. **He**, **she**, **it**, **we**, and **they** are pronouns.

Nouns
Cassie went to camp.
The campers had fun.

Pronouns
She went to camp.
They had fun.

Draw lines from the nouns to the pronouns that can take their place.

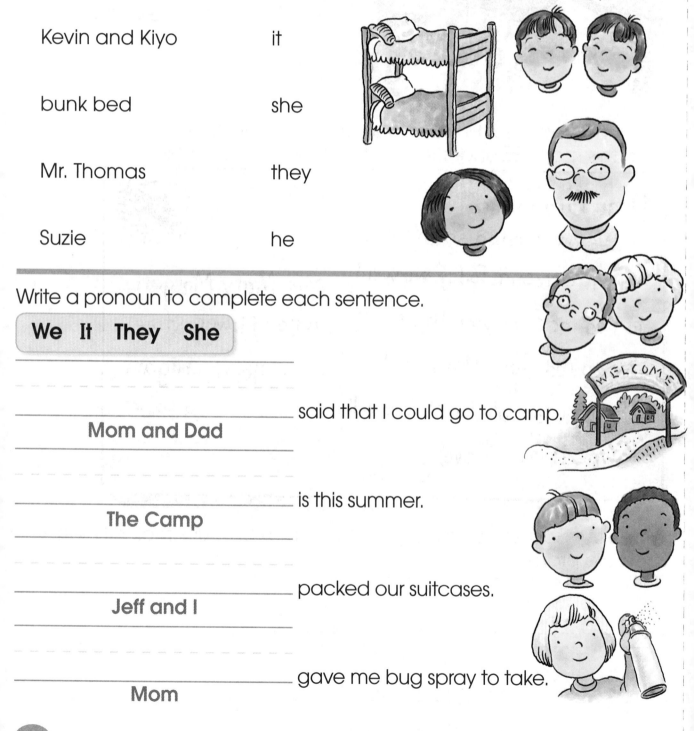

Kevin and Kiyo   it

bunk bed   she

Mr. Thomas   they

Suzie   he

Write a pronoun to complete each sentence.

We   It   They   She

_____ said that I could go to camp.
Mom and Dad

_____ is this summer.
The Camp

_____ packed our suitcases.
Jeff and I

_____ gave me bug spray to take.
Mom

I and Me

I is a subject pronoun that takes the place of your name. **Me** is an object pronoun that takes the place of your name. When you write about another person and yourself, always name yourself last.

> **Mom and I** picked out our new computer.
> Mom taught **me** to use the computer.

Write **I** or **me** to complete each sentence.

_____

_____ thought using a computer would be hard.

_____

It took _____ three hours to learn.

_____

But mom made it easy for _____.

_____

She taught _____ how to write things.

_____

My mom says she will teach _____ how to work with pictures.

_____

_____ am lucky to have a techie mom.

A **verb** is an **action word** that tells what someone or something does.

run   jump   laugh   cry   eat   sleep

Read the sentences.
Write the verbs.

Let's play ball. _____

Jake hits the ball. _____

The ball flies high. _____

Wen runs after it. _____

Will she catch it? _____

Will Wen drop the ball? _____

Look at the word box. Circle the action words in the puzzle.

jog run hop dig fly
jump kick skip swing

```
r w s k i p k f c
u m c z q f k p l
n k z s w i n g t
m n r d c q z p j
d w f l y z h o p
i v l m d q a p v
g c x p f k i c k
v z j u m p w g n
v s p q z l j o g
```

Find the Action Words

As you've learned, a verb is a word that tells about an action. Verbs tell what somebody is doing or what is happening.

Frogs **hop**.
People **walk**.

Underline the verb in each sentence.

Four geese jump in the water.

They paddle with their feet.

The geese swim across the pond.

They flap their wings.

Then they fly away.

Write a verb to complete each sentence.

climb   search   catch

Bears _____ for food in forests.

They can _____ trees.

They can also _____ fish.

Can You Catch the Action Words?

Read the sentences.

Kangaroos hop. Lions stalk.
Snakes glide. People walk.

The words **hop**, **stalk**, **glide**, and **walk** are verbs.

Underline the verb in each sentence.
Write the verbs on the lines.

_____

Monkeys swing from tree to tree. _____

Zebras roam in herds. _____

Tigers hide in tall grasses. _____

Lizards crawl under rocks. _____

Write the verb that best completes each sentence.

jump   run   eat

_____

Deer _____ plants in the forest.

These animals _____ on the ground.

They can also _____ over fences.

Ready, Set, Waddle!

Read the story.
Underline the verbs.

Five ducks waddle to the pond.

They jump into the cool water.

They paddle with their feet.

They dive under the water.

They bob back up.

They swim to the other side.

Then they fly away.

Circle the verbs that tell what the ducks did.

How do the ducks get to the pond?	walk	waddle
How do they get into the cool water?	jump	hop
How do they get to the other side?	slide	swim
How do they leave?	fly	jog

Puppy Power!

Read the poem.
Underline the verbs.

She dashes and darts,

Scrambles and slides,

Bumps into walls,

Rolls on her sides,

Pounces on balls,

Leaps on the chair,

Spins round and round,

Pops up on the chair.

Then she sits.

Write a sentence using the verb "slides."

_____

_____

_____

_____

Write a sentence using the verb "flops."

_____

_____

_____

_____

Present Tense

Some verbs tell about an action that happens now.
Add **s** to a verb that tells what one person, animal, or thing does.

A monkey **howls** out loud.
The other monkeys **howl** back.

Write a verb to complete each sentence.

Noisy birds _____ in the trees.
sit   sits

A jaguar _____ for food.
hunt   hunts

The monkey _____ upside down.
hang   hangs

Giant snakes _____ along the river.
glide   glides

A bat _____ down to catch bugs.
swoop   swoops

The parrots _____ fruit.
eat   eats

Past Tense

Verbs can tell about an action that happened in the past.
Many verbs add **ed** to tell about the past.

Some dinosaurs **walked** on the ground.
Others **climbed** over rocks.

Draw a line from each verb that tells about now
to the matching verb that tells about the past.

work	washed
play	worked
wash	waited
wait	liked
like	played

Write a verb to complete each sentence.

looked   chased   walked   played

Monday, we _____ to the beach.

We _____ for shells.

We _____ in the sand.

Our dog _____ seagulls.

Verbs: Is, Are, and Were

The verbs **is** and **are** tell what things are like now.

That clown **is** silly.
Those clowns **are** silly.
The clowns are silly now.

The verbs **was** and **were** tell what things were like in the past.

That clown **was** sad.
Those clowns **were** sad.
The clowns were sad in the past.

Write **is**, **are**, **was**, or **were** to complete each sentence.

A backyard circus _____ fun.

My dog _____ barking now.

My sisters _____ happy to be clowns.

My parents _____ laughing and clapping.

Last year, my brother _____ scared of clowns.

The clowns _____ too loud for him back then.

Verbs: Has, Have, and Had

The verbs **has** and **have** tell about an action that is happening now.

Use **has** with words that mean one person or thing.

Our community **has** a new school.

Use **have** with I, you, and words that name more than one person or thing.

I **have** a new class this year.

The verb **had** tells about the past.

Last year, we **had** music class.

Write **has**, **have**, or **had** to complete each sentence.

Our new school _____ a huge gym.

Last year, we _____ no gym.

We also _____ a great gym teacher now.

We _____ fun and learn a lot from him.

We _____ a different gym teacher last year.

Our class always _____ a great time.

Describing Words

An adjective can describe a noun.
An adjective can tell how many or what kind.

I have <u>two</u> dogs.
I saw a <u>tall</u> giraffe.

Read the sentences.
Underline the adjectives.
Draw lines from the sentences to the cats they describe.

Lady is a big cat.

She had three kittens.

Tiger is the striped kitten.

Jet is the black kitten.

The little kitten is Socks.

We now have four cats.

Warm Weather

An adjective can describe how things taste or feel.

> hot   cold   loud   wet   quiet   soft

Write the correct adjectives to finish the sentences.

_____

The sun is _____.

_____

A jet makes a _____ sound.

_____

Ice cream is _____.

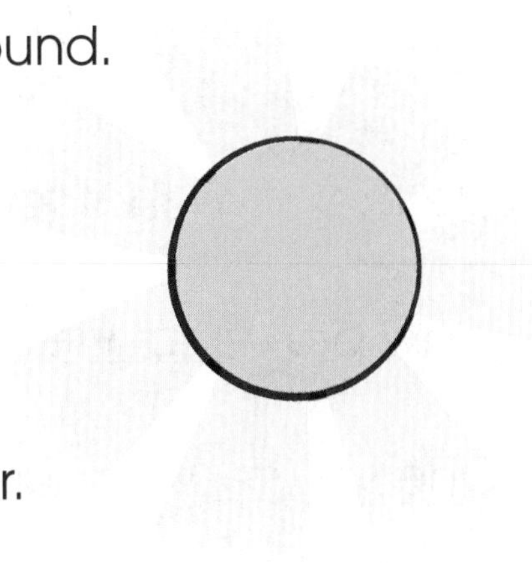

_____

The kitten has _____ fur.

_____

Don't slip on the _____ grass.

_____

The _____ deer hides.

Squirrel Chase

An adjective tells about a noun.
Remember: Nouns are words that name people, animals, places, or things.

Circle the word that tells about the underlined noun.

I saw brown <u>squirrels</u> at the park.

One <u>squirrel</u> was burying little <u>nuts</u>.

A big <u>dog</u> ran after it.

Two <u>squirrels</u> ran up a tall <u>tree</u>.

The green <u>leaves</u> hid them from sight.

Write two of the adjectives.

_____

_____

_____

_____

Doghouse

Read the story.
Underline the adjectives.

I have a big dog.

Anna has a small dog.

My dog has long fur.

Anna's dog has short fur.

Both dogs have green collars.

Our dogs are great pets.

Circle the correct answers to the questions.

What kind of pets do dogs make?	bad	fine	great
What color are the dogs' collars?	red	green	blue
Which adjective is the opposite of "big"?	long	green	small
Which adjective is the opposite of "short"?	small	long	great

Write about a dog you would like to have.
Use adjectives such as its color and size.

_____

_____

_____

_____

_____

_____

Do Bugs Bug You?

An adjective can tell how someone or something acts, sounds, feels, smells, or tastes.

The **hard** shell of a beetle protects it.
A cricket makes **loud** chirping sounds.
A grasshopper has **long** legs.

snapping   beautiful   zigzag   fast   smelly   stubby

Write an adjective to describe the insect in each sentence.

A butterfly is a _____ insect.

Caterpillars have _____ feet.

A beetle's click is a _____ sound.

The tiger beetle is a _____ runner.

The whirligig beetle makes _____ patterns when it swims.

The stinkbug gives off a _____ odor if it is bothered.

Little Ladybugs

An adjective is a describing word. It tells about a noun.
An adjective can be a number, size, or color.
An adjective can tell how something looks, sounds, or feels.
Many adjectives come before the nouns they describe.

There are many ladybugs in the garden. "Many" is an adjective.

Read the story.
Underline the adjectives.

A ladybug is a small beetle.

It has a round body.

It may have red or orange wings.

The wings have black spots.

This tiny insect helps people.

Ladybugs eat harmful insects.

Circle the nouns that the adjectives describe.

"Small" describes	wings	beetle
"Red or orange" describes	wings	body
"Round" describes	body	spots
"Harmful" describes	wings	insects

Marching Band

Every year on July 4, there is a parade.
These words describe things in the parade:

| Six loud shiny tall pretty blue furry big |

Describing words are called adjectives. Adjectives describe nouns. Some adjectives tell how things sound, look, or feel. Write adjectives from the box to finish the sentences.

_____   _____

A _____ man in a _____ hat leads the parade.

_____   _____

_____ musicians march in their _____ uniforms.

_____   _____

A _____ girl plays a _____ horn.

_____   _____

The _____ drum makes a _____ sound.

Fast, Faster, Fastest!

Add **er** to a word to make it mean more.
Add **est** to a word to make it mean the most.

| longest   longer   fast   faster   fastest |

Write the word that belongs in each sentence.

_____

Tiger's tail is _____ than a rabbit's tail.

_____

Monkey's tail is the _____ of all.

_____

Mouse was the _____ runner.

_____

"Mouse can run very _____," said Tiger.

_____

Monkey ran _____ than rabbit.

High, Higher, Highest

Add **er** to some adjectives to compare two people, animals, places, or things.

Add **est** to some adjectives to compare more than two nouns.

Write the adjectives using **er** or **est**.

Debby's baton is (high) than Gail's.

_____

_____

Perri's baton is the (high) of all three.

_____

_____

The (smooth) twirler on the team is Gail.

_____

_____

Debby is a (fast) twirler than Perri.

_____

_____

Perri is (old) than Debby.

_____

Camping Trip

The **subject** of a sentence tells who or what the sentence is about.
<u>My family</u> went on a trip.
"My family" tells who this sentence is about.

<u>The trip</u> took six hours.
"The trip" tells what this sentence is about.

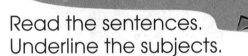

Read the sentences.
Underline the subjects.

Then circle who or what.

Our family visited Yellowstone National Park.	who	what
The park has lakes and springs.	who	what
People camp in the park.	who	what
Stars fill the night sky.	who	what
Forests are everywhere.	who	what
Hikers climb hills.	who	what

Write subjects to finish the sentences.

_____

_____ is fun to visit.

_____

_____ and I go there a lot.

Wise Owl

The **predicate** of a sentence includes a verb and tells more about what the subject does.

Birds <u>make nests</u>.

Read the sentences.
Underline the predicates.

Owls hunt at night.

Elk eat green plants.

Eagles nest in the park.

Water shoots up from underground.

Hikers walk down trails.

The forest is quiet.

Write predicates to finish the sentences.

_____

Campers _____

_____

A squirrel _____

Time to Paint

A **contraction** is a short way to write two words.

I am → I'm

Write a contraction for the underlined words.

haven't	don't	let's	can't	aren't	won't

Please <u>do not</u> go. _____

We <u>are not</u> done. _____

We <u>have not</u> painted it. _____

<u>Let us</u> paint it red. _____

It <u>will not</u> take long. _____

I <u>can not</u> paint without a paint brush. _____

Noisy Parade

A contraction is a short way to write two words.
An **apostrophe** (') shows where one or more letters have been left out.
In some contractions, the **o** in **not** is removed.

do not → don't	can not → can't	will not → won't

Draw lines from the words to the matching contractions.

will not	isn't
is not	won't
can not	can't
do not	doesn't
does not	don't

Write a contraction to complete each sentence.

Dana _____ like parades.
does not

I _____ think she will go.
do not

She _____ enjoy the band.
will not

My sister _____ going, either.
is not

Quiet Garden

As you've learned, a contraction is a short way to write two words. An apostrophe (') takes the place of the missing letter or letters.

are not → aren't   **what is → what's**

A guide is talking to a class about Green Gardens. Write contractions from the box to finish the sentences. Below each sentence, write the words that make each contraction.

> **I'm   There's   We'll**

_____

_____ a lot to see at Green Gardens.

_____   _____

_____ + _____

_____

_____ sure the class will enjoy our day.

_____   _____

_____ + _____

_____

_____ visit the rainforest and desert areas.

_____   _____

_____ + _____

You're Learning to Read

Write the contractions to finish the sentences.

I'll   aren't   couldn't   We're   isn't   they're   can't   don't   they'll

_____

I _____ find my book.
could not

Dad _____ find his watch.
cannot

They said _____ meet us there.
they will

_____ get the pizza for the party.
I will

It _____ time for the bus.
is not

_____ all tired from our soccer game.
We are

They _____ want to come with us.
do not

Our dogs _____ going with us.
are not

Who said _____ on the way back?
they are

© School Zone Publishing Company 06345

Making One Word Out of Two

Two words that are put together to make one word become a **compound word**.

skate + board = skateboard

| rainbow | cupcake | birdhouse | football | butterfly |

Write the compound words.

_____

_____

_____

_____

_____

Draw a line to divide each compound word.

s t a r f i s h   r a t t l e s n a k e

Putting Words Together

Look at the pictures.
Write the compound words on the lines.

> sunflower   starfish   firefly   skateboard
> rattlesnake   basketball   doghouse

Words are Everywhere!

Circle the two words in each compound word.

something   snowball

everywhere   anyone

inside   cannot

maybe   sunshine

herself   birthday

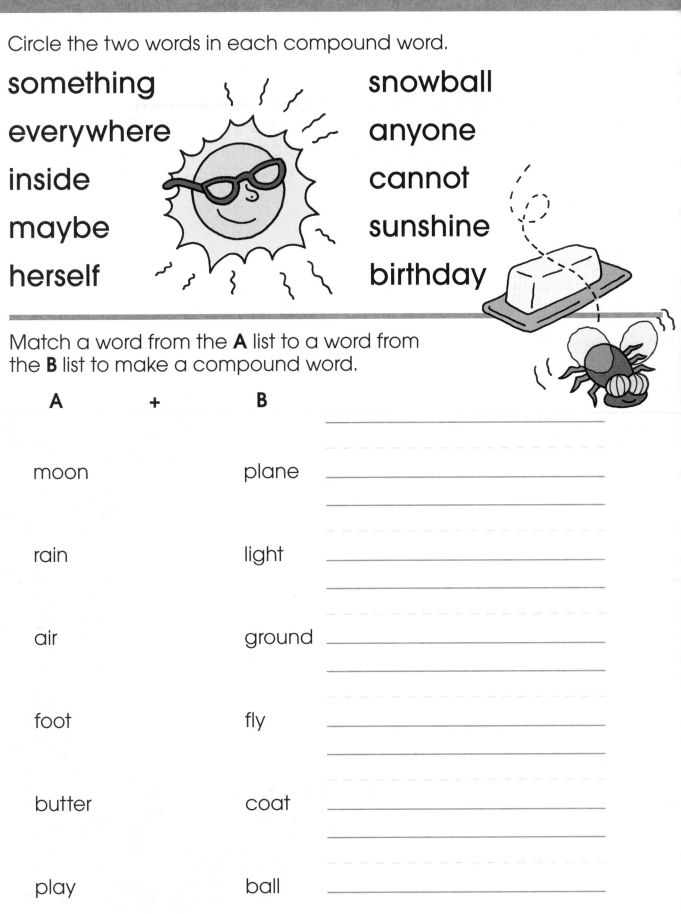

Match a word from the **A** list to a word from the **B** list to make a compound word.

A	+	B	
moon		plane	
rain		light	
air		ground	
foot		fly	
butter		coat	
play		ball	

In the Rainforest Garden

Read the paragraph. Underline the compound words.
Then write the words that make the compound words.

     When they got to the greenhouses, the class visited
the rainforest area. Everyone looked around. They took their
notebooks from their backpacks. Someone began drawing the
banana plant. Somebody else asked questions about the plant.

_____   _____

_____ + _____

_____

_____ + _____

_____

_____ + _____

_____

_____ + _____

_____

_____ + _____

_____

_____ + _____

_____ + _____

To, Two, or Too?

Homophones are words that sound alike but are spelled differently. They also have different meanings.

Write the correct homophone to finish each sentence.

Give the toy _____ the baby.

           to two

Put the book over _____.

           their there

I cannot _____ her.

           hear here

Who _____ the game?

           won one

Is your answer _____ ?

           write right

I saw a _____ at the petting zoo.

           dear deer

I See the Bright Blue Sea

Write the correct homophone to finish each sentence.

I can't stay up late at _____.

night   knight

A letter came for me in the _____.

mail   male

There is a _____ in my sock!

whole   hole

Can you count to _____?

for   four

Jan _____ the apple.

ate   eight

I braid my _____ every morning.

hair   hare

My Aunt is Not an Ant

The bear had a stubby **tail**.
<u>Goldilocks and the Three Bears</u> is a **tale**.
Tail and **tale** sound the same, but they have different meanings. A tail is a part of an animal's body, and a tale is a story.

Write the correct homophone to finish each sentence.

_____   _____

Our team _____ the game by _____ point.
          one   won   one   won

We _____ down a country _____ .
      road   rode   road   rode

Let's go _____ the library at _____ o'clock.
            to   two   to   two

_____ you help me stack this _____ ?
   Wood   Would   wood   would

I _____ I'd get a _____ bike for my birthday.
    new   knew   new   knew

House and Home

Synonyms are words with almost the same meaning (**look**, **see**).

Write the synonym for the bold word in each sentence.

| noisy | harm | solid | roast |
| speak | quiet | welcome | jolly |

Everyone was in a **merry** mood.

_____

It was a **still** summer evening.

_____

The fall did not **hurt** her.

_____

The crowd became very **loud**.

_____

It is time to **bake** the turkey.

_____

The peach felt **firm**.

_____

Did Mr. James **talk** to your class?

_____

She went to the door to **greet** him.

_____

© School Zone Publishing Company 06345

Tiny or Huge?

Antonyms are words with opposite meanings (**big**, **little**).

Write the antonym for the bold word in each sentence.

laugh	sour	short	easy
start	lose	dirty	slow

My father is a **tall** man.

_____

Did you **find** your money?

_____

It is time to **stop** the game.

_____

The lemonade is too **sweet**.

_____

The story made him **cry**.

_____

I thought the test was **hard**.

_____

The horse was **fast**.

_____

Is your shirt **clean**?

_____

It's Raining Cats and Dogs

Idioms are expressions or phrases that do not mean what they seem to say.

"**You crack me up!**" means "**you make me laugh.**"

Draw a line to match each idiom with its meaning.

all tied up	flatter
butter up	be quiet
a piece of cake	make every effort
walking on air	tell a secret
bend over backwards	easy
bite your tongue	get angry
top banana	asleep
blow your top	lead person
spill the beans	busy
out like a light	happy

Alphabetical order is the order of the letters in the alphabet. These words are in alphabetical order.

ant   **b**lue   **d**ing

When words start with the same letter, use the second letter to put them in alphabetical order.

pig   **pl**ant   **pu**mpkin

Look at the sets of books. Use the **author's last name** to number them 1, 2, 3, and 4 in alphabetical order. The first set is done for you.

Snake Hunt by H.S. Fang — 3

Cub Kitchen by Ted E. Bear — 1

Cats and Dogs by Red Setter — 4

Bee Attack! by Hy Bumble — 2

Racing for Fun by Howie Fast

Swimming Tips by Lee Lake

Home Run! by Ima Hitter

Gymnastics by Flip N. Jump

Mountain Trail by Oma Blisters

Jungle Trek by Annie Body

Oceans Away by C. Breeze

Desert Heat by Sandy Beach

Wonderful Words

Some words have more than one meaning.
A dictionary numbers each meaning.

Read the definition of **plant**.

> **plant** 1. any living thing that can make its own food from sunlight, air, and water 2. to put in the ground and grow

Read each sentence.
Write the number of the correct meaning.

a. Where should we plant the rose bush? _____

b. The plant needs water. _____

Read the definition of **bulb**.

> **bulb** 1. a hollow glass light that glows when electricity is turned on 2. a round bud or stem that you can plant in the ground

Read each sentence. Write the number of the correct meaning.

c. Oh, no! I think the bulb burned out. _____

d. Plant the tulip bulb in the garden. _____

Table of Contents

Kim and LaTasha want to learn more about cactuses. They choose a book about their subject. They read the contents page to find out what information is in the book.

Contents

To which pages would you turn to find:

what kind of cactus the girls saw in the greenhouse?

_____

_____

the name of the sharp parts of a cactus?

_____

_____

how cactuses grow?

_____

_____

another book about cactuses?

_____

_____

how cactuses are used in medicine?

_____

_____

What would be a good title for this book?

_____

_____

Fact or Opinion?

A **fact** is something that can be proved.

Birds have wings.
You can look at a bird or check in a book to find out whether birds have wings.

An **opinion** is something that someone believes. An opinion can't be proved.

A robin is pretty.

Circle **fact** or **opinion**.

Most birds can fly.	fact	opinion
Birds make good pets.	fact	opinion
Birds lay eggs.	fact	opinion
Owls are smart.	fact	opinion
Robins make the best nests.	fact	opinion
Most birds have feathers.	fact	opinion

Write one fact about birds.

_____

_____

What is your opinion about birds?

_____

_____

_____

_____

Fish Go Swish, Swish

Circle fact or opinion.

Most ocean animals are fish.	fact	opinion
Fish make good pets.	fact	opinion
Some fish have bright colors.	fact	opinion
Fish are cold-blooded.	fact	opinion
Fishing is fun.	fact	opinion
Everyone should eat fish.	fact	opinion

Write one fact about fish.

_____

_____

What is your opinion about fish?

_____

_____

_____

_____

Help for a Sick Pig

Read the sentences. Circle yes if they are true. Circle no if they are not true. Circle the letters next to your answers. Then write the circled letters in order on the blanks below to answer the riddle.

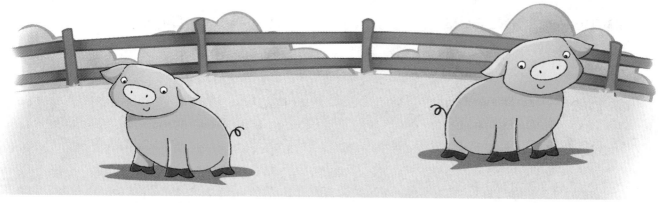

Celery is a vegetable.	yes o	no g
Birds fly.	yes i	no j
The letters **a**, **e**, **i**, **o**, and **u** are consonants.	yes s	no n
"Each," "eat," and "bead" have the **long a** sound.	yes w	no k
"Happy" is the opposite of "sad."	yes m	no r
Bees make honey.	yes e	no l
"Same" is a synonym of "different."	yes k	no n
"King" and "ring" are rhyming words.	yes t	no q

What do you give sick pigs?

___ ___ ___ ___ ___ ___ ___ ___

___ ___ ___ ___ ___ ___ ___ ___

3 Feet

Read the sentences. Circle yes if they are true. Circle no if they are not true. Circle the letters next to your answers. Then write the circled letters in order on the blanks below to answer the riddle.

All birds have feathers.	yes	y	no	g
All living things need food.	yes	a	no	l
Insects have bones.	yes	w	no	r
Ice is frozen water.	yes	d	no	f
Trees are large plants.	yes	s	no	r
Plants need water to grow.	yes	t	no	s
The world's largest animal is the giraffe.	yes	v	no	i
The earth is flat.	yes	i	no	c
A plant is alive.	yes	k	no	x

What has a foot on each side and one in the middle?

____ ____ ____ ____ ____ ____ ____ ____ ____

A ____ ____ ____ ____ ____ ____ ____ ____

Why Did This Happen?

The snowman is melting.

Why did this happen?

The sun came out and the temperature rose.

The sun and the rising temperature **caused** the snowman to melt.
The **effect** of the sun and the rising temperature is the melting snowman.

Read the effect. Write the cause.

The dog is eating.

Why did this happen?

_____

_____

_____

_____

What Will Happen Next?

Put check marks by what you think will happen next.

The baby is hungry.

☐ The baby is given a toy.

☐ The baby is given dinner.

The family dog is lost.

☐ The family looks for it.

☐ The family watches TV.

It begins to rain at the picnic.

☐ The family eats.

☐ The family packs up and leaves.

The car has a flat tire.

☐ The tire is fixed.

☐ The car is sold.

Bill's shirt is torn.

☐ Bill wears the torn shirt.

☐ Bill puts on a new shirt.

Asking Questions

Asking the questions "who," "what," "where," "when," "why," and "how" can help you understand a story.

Read the story below.
Answer the questions.

Tomorrow is Katie's birthday party. She is excited. Katie and her friend Lauren are going to ride the bus to the zoo. Katie wants to see the monkeys first because they are her favorite animal. After the zoo, Katie will have a pizza party at home and open her presents. It will be so much fun. She can't wait.

Who is having a birthday party?

_____

_____

What will Katie do after the zoo?

_____

_____

When is Katie's party?

_____

_____

Where is Katie's party?

Why does Katie want to see the monkeys first?

How will Katie and Lauren get to the zoo?

What is the best title for this story? Circle it.

Katie's Pizza Party

Monkeys and Pizza

Katie's Exciting Birthday Party

Create your own title for this story.

Real or Make-Believe?

Real things can actually happen.
Make-believe things cannot really happen.

Circle real or make-believe.

The cow jumped over the moon.	real	make-believe
Jenny fed the cow hay.	real	make-believe
The cat looks for mice in the barn.	real	make-believe
The cat came dancing out of the barn.	real	make-believe
An old woman lives near us.	real	make-believe
An old woman lives in a shoe.	real	make-believe
Three little kittens lost their mittens.	real	make-believe
Three little kittens were lost.	real	make-believe

Reality or Fantasy?

Reality stories are about things that have or could really happen.
Fantasy stories are about things that could not really happen.

Reality story

Fantasy story

Write **R** in front of what could really happen.
Write **F** in front of what could not really happen.

_____ The pig spread his wings and flew away.

_____ The fireman rushed to put out the fire.

_____ The fox had a party with the chicken.

_____ Sea turtles laid their eggs on the beach.

_____ The dish ran away with the spoon.

_____ The farmer planted gumball trees.

_____ Dad rowed the boat across the river.

_____ The baby played with toy animals.

Rainforest Stories

Read about Green Gardens' rainforest area.
Then answer the questions.

Martin and Lee saw something moving in the grass. They heard a peeping sound. The boys ran to see what was making the noise. The guide walked over. "That's a baby quail," she said.

What is a quail?

_____

_____

_____

_____

"This area had too many ants," the guide told us. "Quail like to eat ants. That gave us an idea. Now our problem is solved."

What was the problem?

_____

_____

_____

_____

How was the problem solved?

_____

_____

_____

_____

The guide showed the students some bamboo. Bamboo is a kind of giant grass with a hollow stem. Bamboo can grow as much as 6 inches in one day. Some bamboo grow as high as 120 feet. That's taller than 24 men standing on each other's shoulders!

Does bamboo grow faster or slower than most plants?

_____

_____

What is one big difference between grass in a lawn and bamboo?

_____

_____

In the tropics, or hot places on Earth, some people live in bamboo houses and use bamboo furniture. Their mats, baskets, animal pens, and boats are made from bamboo. Bamboo shades their yards.

Sum it up. Why is bamboo so important to people in the tropics?

_____

_____

_____

_____

_____

Rosy R Words

Circle the words in the word search.

RAIN   RING   ROBOT   ROSE   RUG   RED   ROBIN   ROPE

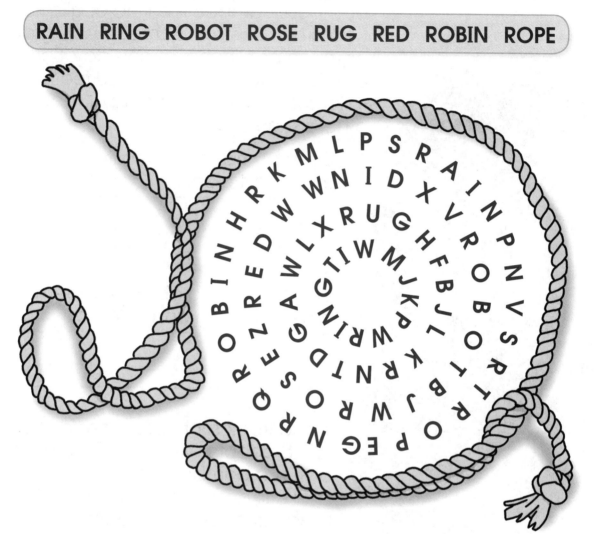

Write the words as you find them in the puzzle.

Animal Word Search

Circle the words in the word search.

PANDA   SEAL   BEAR   TIGER   ZEBRA   LION   ELEPHANT

```
G  P  A  N  D  A  P  D  A
J  X  S  Z  W  T  W  J  B
T  Q  K  S  E  A  L  C  E
I  U  Z  C  Q  M  P  B  A
G  P  Z  E  B  R  A  Z  R
E  Q  H  K  J  X  J  T  R
R  R  X  L  I  O  N  Y  U
K  B  Z  X  T  P  M  X  W
V  E  L  E  P  H  A  N  T
```

Write sentences using as many words from the puzzle as you can.

_____

_____

_____

_____

_____

_____

_____

Flower Power

Circle the words in the word search.

FLOWERS   SEEDS   WATER   SUN   ROOTS   SOIL

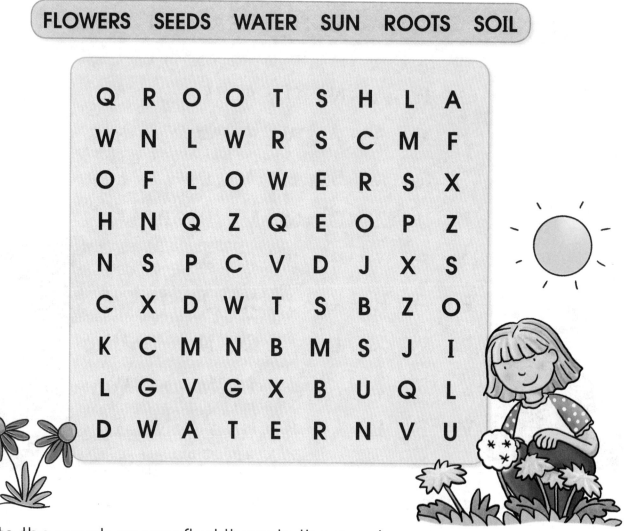

Q R O O T S H L A
W N L W R S C M F
O F L O W E R S X
H N Q Z Q E O P Z
N S P C V D J X S
C X D W T S B Z O
K C M N B M S J I
L G V G X B U Q L
D W A T E R N V U

Write the words as you find them in the puzzle.

_____   _____

_____   _____

_____   _____

_____   _____

_____   _____

Shape Word Search

Circle the words in the word search.

TRIANGLE SQUARE DIAMOND STAR RECTANGLE OVAL CIRCLE

A	M	C	Z	X	W	T	U	R
F	D	I	A	M	O	N	D	E
G	P	R	W	P	Q	N	X	C
R	A	C	O	V	A	L	S	T
O	Z	L	V	F	G	S	Q	A
A	S	E	Z	P	X	K	U	N
J	T	T	B	S	R	C	A	G
K	A	Z	B	C	D	V	R	L
T	R	I	A	N	G	L	E	E

Write sentences using as many words from the puzzle as you can.

_____

_____

_____

_____

_____

_____

_____

Building Vocabulary

Transportation Word Search

Circle the words in the word search.

CAR   TRUCK   BIKE   TRAIN   BUS   VAN   PLANE

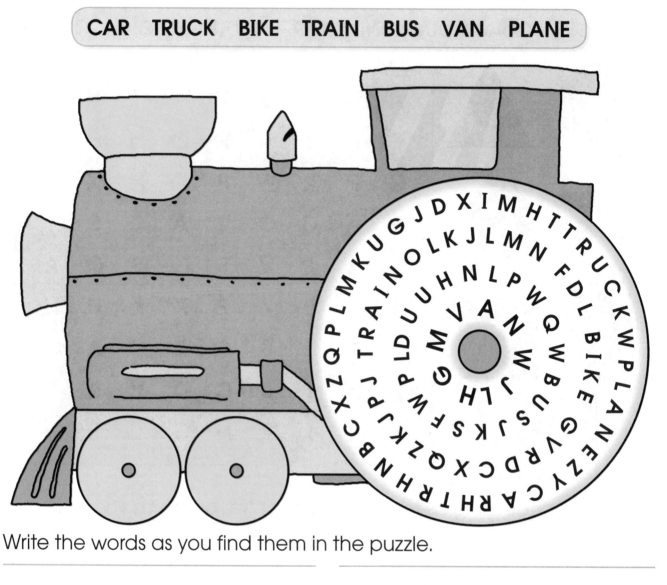

Write the words as you find them in the puzzle.

_____   _____

_____   _____

_____   _____

_____   _____

_____   _____

What Day is Today?

Circle the words in the word search.

**MONDAY   TUESDAY   WEDNESDAY   THURSDAY
FRIDAY   SATURDAY   SUNDAY**

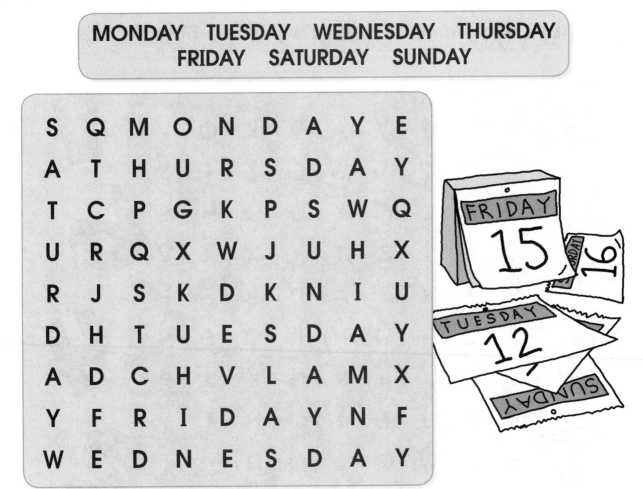

```
S  Q  M  O  N  D  A  Y  E
A  T  H  U  R  S  D  A  Y
T  C  P  G  K  P  S  W  Q
U  R  Q  X  W  J  U  H  X
R  J  S  K  D  K  N  I  U
D  H  T  U  E  S  D  A  Y
A  D  C  H  V  L  A  M  X
Y  F  R  I  D  A  Y  N  F
W  E  D  N  E  S  D  A  Y
```

Write sentences using as many words from the puzzle as you can.

_____

_____

_____

_____

_____

_____

_____

Number Word Search

Circle the words in the word search.

ONE   TWO   THREE   FOUR   FIVE   SIX   SEVEN   EIGHT

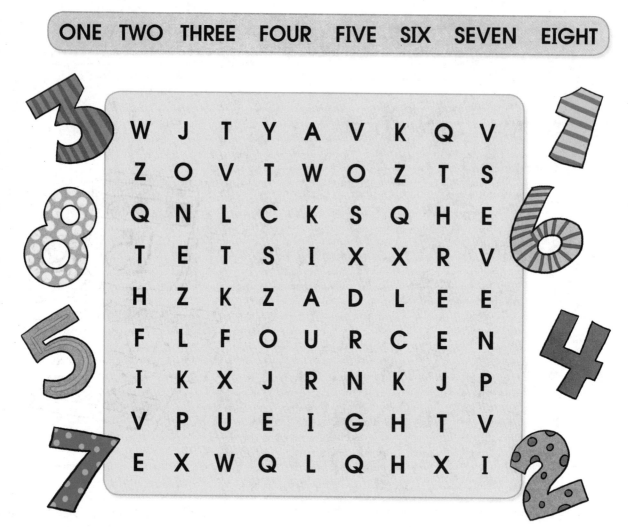

```
W  J  T  Y  A  V  K  Q  V
Z  O  V  T  W  O  Z  T  S
Q  N  L  C  K  S  Q  H  E
T  E  T  S  I  X  X  R  V
H  Z  K  Z  A  D  L  E  E
F  L  F  O  U  R  C  E  N
I  K  X  J  R  N  K  J  P
V  P  U  E  I  G  H  T  V
E  X  W  Q  L  Q  H  X  I
```

Write the words as you find them in the puzzle.

_____   _____

_____   _____

_____   _____

_____   _____

_____   _____

_____   _____

Giant Reading Readiness **06345**